*English Phonetic Texts*

# ENGLISH PHONETIC TEXTS

by

## DAVID ABERCROMBIE

Professor of Phonetics
Edinburgh University

FABER AND FABER LTD

24 Russell Square

London

*First published in mcmlxiv*
*by Faber and Faber Limited*
*24 Russell Square, London, W.C.1*
*Printed in Great Britain by*
*Western Printing Services Limited, Bristol*

# Acknowledgments

Acknowledgments and thanks are due to the following for permission to reproduce extracts from copyright works in the texts included in this book: The Regents of the University of Wisconsin for *Prolegomena to a Theory of Language* by Louis Hjelmslev; T. S. Eliot and Messrs. Faber and Faber Ltd. for 'Poetry and Drama' from *On Poetry and Poets*; Messrs. Routledge and Kegan Paul for 'The Problem of Meaning in Primitive Languages' by B. Malinowski and for *The Spirit of Language in Civilisation* by Karl Vossler; Messrs. Doubleday and Company, Inc., and Messrs. Hodder and Stoughton Ltd. for *The Story of My Life* by Helen Keller; the British Academy for 'Spoken and Written Language' from *Proceedings of the British Academy*, volume VI; Mrs. Lascelles Abercrombie for *The Theory of Poetry* by Lascelles Abercrombie; The Public Trustee and The Society of Authors for *Pygmalion* by Bernard Shaw; Mr. David Lloyd-James, and Messrs. Routledge and Kegan Paul Ltd. for *The Broadcast Word* by A. Lloyd James; Mrs. Dorothée Anderson for *A Few Documents on English Phonetic Notation* by Harold E. Palmer.

# Contents

# Contents

# *Foreword*

This collection of transcribed texts was put together to meet the needs of students taking the courses given in the Department of Phonetics of the University of Edinburgh; it is hoped, however, that it will prove of interest to others as well. Many of my colleagues have been kind enough to read the book in manuscript; among them I am particularly indebted to Dr. Peter Ladefoged and Professor Peter Strevens for a number of suggestions, and my very special thanks are due to Miss Lindsay Criper, whose assistance with every aspect of the book has been invaluable. I am most grateful to Miss Mary Macintyre for the care she has taken in typing a difficult manuscript.

*Edinburgh*                                                        D.A.

# Part I

INTRODUCTION

# Introduction

**i The present series of texts**

The principal object of this book is to provide a selection of English texts transcribed phonetically in a style of transcription which, though quite widely used, has not up to now been available in an English phonetic reader.[1] The phonetic symbols are those of the International Phonetic Association,[2] and they are used in accordance with the Association's principles. The book also provides, in Appendix I, an opportunity of comparing this sort of transcription with a number of other ways of transcribing English, all of which are in conformity with the principles of the IPA (for there is no such thing as *the* IPA transcription of English, in the sense of an officially sanctioned variety). The various factors on which the differences between these other modes of transcription depend are discussed at some length in this Introduction.

There are many collections of English phonetic texts already in existence. These collections offer the student a wide variety of choice in the sort of reading matter of which the texts consist, in the styles of delivery which are chosen, and (though here one could wish the variety was a great deal wider) in the kinds of accent which the transcriptions represent. It will be generally agreed that it is an excellent thing to have such variety available to students. It is less likely to be generally agreed, however, that the equally wide variety of *types of transcription* used in these phonetic readers is a good thing. The lack of unanimity among

[1] Orthographic versions of the texts are given in Appendix II.
[2] Hereafter referred to as the IPA.

13

phoneticians in their transcriptions of English is, in fact, often deplored by foreign teachers of the language, who complain that, for example, the number of different symbols for vowels in existing published texts may be as few as seven, or as many as fifteen, and there may or may not be a length-mark as well. Nevertheless, I believe that variety is a good thing here too. Phonetic texts are required for many different purposes and for various types of audience. A mode of transcription which is satisfactory in one case will not necessarily be satisfactory in another, and it is not, in the nature of things, possible for a 'standard' mode of transcription of English, suitable for all purposes and all audiences, to be agreed on by phoneticians. The type of transcription employed in the present work is probably not a good one for teaching English pronunciation to foreign learners who are beginning work on the language, and it is not for them that these texts are intended. On the other hand it is a type of transcription which is well suited to teaching general phonetics, and the phonetics of the mother-tongue, to native English-speaking students; and experience has shown it to be valuable also for use in discussion of problems of the spoken language with advanced foreign specialists in English. I believe, indeed, that it is better fitted to these purposes than are any of the other types of transcription at present available in phonetic readers (the great majority of which are designed for foreign learners of English). I therefore make no apology for adding yet one more to the types of transcription used for connected phonetic texts in English. The present collection of texts, since it is addressed to a different audience, does not compete with other collections.

The transcription of the texts is based on the accent of Standard English[1] which is best called 'RP', or 'Received Pronunciation'.[2] RP is, within England, a non-regional accent; other

---

[1] For the sense in which the terms 'accent' and 'Standard English' are used, see David Abercrombie, *Problems and Principles* (London, 1956), Ch. IV.

[2] This term has been current since the middle of the nineteenth century; the word 'received' has the meaning 'socially received', 'acceptable in good society'. The conveniently neutral abbreviation 'RP' seems to have been

educated accents all have local characteristics. It is, however, perfectly possible to interpret this transcription in terms of other educated accents whose local characteristics are not too marked. There are, as a matter of fact, a number of educated accents of England which have the same system of phonemes as RP, fairly similar phonetic realization of the phonemes, and few differences of phonemic distribution. The transcription fits these accents equally well.

The sounds of RP have been very fully described by a number of writers, and it is assumed here that readers of these texts will be familiar with the content of these descriptions. Daniel Jones's *Pronunciation of English*, 4th edition (1956), will give all the information necessary to the accurate interpretation of the texts.

The consonant symbols of these transcribed texts are those generally found in IPA transcriptions of English. They are as follows (all phonetic symbols in this Introduction appear in sans serif type):

| | | | |
|---|---|---|---|
| p | as in ˈplɛʒə pleasure | r | as in ˈbrʌðə brother |
| b | as in ˈbrʌðə brother | s | as in sʌtʃ such |
| m | as in ˈmɔnɪŋ morning | z | as in zil zeal |
| f | as in fɔ four | ʃ | as in ʃʊə sure |
| v | as in lɪv live | ʒ | as in ˈplɛʒə pleasure |
| θ | as in θɔt thought | k | as in laɪk like |
| ð | as in ˈbrʌðə brother | g | as in gʊ go |
| t | as in taɪm time | ŋ | as in ˈmɔnɪŋ morning |
| d | as in dɑk dark | h | as in hɜd heard |
| n | as in nɒt not | w | as in wɒt what |
| l | as in laɪk like | j | as in jɛs yes |

Syllabic consonants are shown thus: ŋ̩ l̩. tʃ and dʒ are used in tʃɜtʃ church, dʒʌdʒ judge (see below, p. 31).

first used in 1875 by the English phonetician Alexander J. Ellis. A number of other names have at times been given to this accent, and they are often preferred by people who find distasteful the flavour of complacent frankness concerning class barriers which there is about the Victorian term 'received'. Regional names for the accent (such as 'Southern English') are, however, misleading; and it certainly has no right to the label 'British Standard' which is sometimes given to it, particularly by writers in America.

For the representation of vowels the following symbols are used:

| | |
|---|---|
| i as in bid bead | ɜ as in bɜd bird |
| ɪ as in bɪd bid | ə as in ə'baɷt about |
| ɛ as in bɛd bed | eɪ as in deɪ day |
| a as in bad bad | oɷ as in noɷ no |
| ɑ as in bɑd bard | aɪ as in aɪ eye |
| ɒ as in bɒg bog | aɷ as in naɷ now |
| ɔ as in bɔd board | ɒɪ as in bɒɪ boy |
| ɷ as in gɷd good | ɪə as in bɪə beer |
| u as in fud food | ɛə as in bɛə bare |
| ʌ as in bʌd bud | ɷə as in pɷə poor |

It should be noted that no diphthong ɔə exists in my pronunciation.

The length of sounds is not indicated. Stress is shown, in the usual manner, by the mark ' before the stressed syllable; no use has been found for a mark to indicate secondary stress. The punctuation of the original texts has been preserved, and no attempt has been made to indicate intonation. In all cases where distribution differences are found among RP speakers, the pronunciation given in the texts is my own.

A somewhat unfamiliar use of a diacritic is to be found in the transcribed texts: the symbol ə̩ is used, in a way parallel to the use of l̩ and n̩, to indicate, on occasions where there might be doubt, that ə is not the second element of a diphthong but forms a separate syllable. Thus in the word mɪs'tɪərɪə̩s *mysterious* the letters ɪə represent a diphthong the first time they occur, but not the second time. This application of the diacritic does not have explicit IPA sanction, but it seems nevertheless a legitimate and useful extension of its normal use in transcriptions of English.

## ii The classification of types of transcription

A transcription of RP which uses this selection of symbols, in conformity with IPA principles, has usually been called a 'narrow' transcription. However, the traditional terms 'broad' and 'narrow' for types of phonetic transcription are, as is shown below (§ viii), vague and ambiguous, and a more carefully defined set of terms is desirable for occasions when greater precision is needed in classifying transcriptions and describing their characteristics. I have elsewhere[1] put forward such an alternative set of terms, and for convenience they are explained again, at somewhat greater length, here. They are terms which I have found valuable in the teaching of general phonetics, particularly for getting beginners in the subject to think critically about problems of phonetic notation; and valuable also in discussing with foreign teachers the advantages and disadvantages of the many different types of transcription of English.

It is possible to transcribe phonetically any utterance, in any language, in several different ways, all of them using the alphabet and conventions of the IPA. (The same thing is possible with most other 'international' phonetic alphabets.) The difference between these various ways of transcribing may lie in the *shapes of the letters* chosen to represent the sounds, or in the *number of different letters* employed in the transcription. There are thus several types of phonetic transcription, and we can classify them on the basis of these two points of difference. The classification will apply to transcriptions of all languages.

A transcription which is made by using letters of the *simplest possible shapes*, and in the *smallest possible number*, is called a SIMPLE PHONEMIC transcription. It is called 'simple' because of the first characteristic, and 'phonemic' because of the second. An examination of these two characteristics in greater detail will make clear the principles on which simple phonemic transcriptions are based.

### iii  Simple phonemic transcription

*A simple phonemic transcription uses letters of the simplest*

---

[1] In *Le Maître Phonétique*, 1953, p. 32. See also *Orbis*, vol. III, 1954, p. 231. The same classification (in some respects more elaborate) is given by Daniel Jones in his *Outline of English Phonetics*, 8th edition (1956), App. A, and in his *English Pronouncing Dictionary*, 11th edition (1956), p. xviii.

*possible shapes*. This is a typographical principle: the simplest shapes are the most familiar, the most typographically satisfactory, in a word the most 'romanic'.[1] Although it is a typographical principle, it would be pointless if it did not have, as we shall presently see, linguistic implications.

The most familiar, the most typographically satisfactory letter shapes of all, are the *completely* romanic ones—those, that is to say, of the roman alphabet as we know it today. The IPA repertory of phonetic symbols includes all the traditional roman letters. It contains in addition a number of extra letters which have been obtained by modifying roman letters, by borrowing from other alphabets, or by outright invention. These extra letters, such as ŋ ʒ ɯ ʎ, are clearly less romanic in shape, more 'exotic', than the traditional letters of the alphabet. Similarly the addition of diacritics makes ṭ ɬ õ less romanic, more exotic, than t l o.

Among the extra letters, and letters with diacritics, however, some are less foreign to the traditions of the roman alphabet than others are. The former, therefore, though not completely romanic, appear more romanic in comparison with the latter—their shapes seem less strange, and they are more typographically satisfactory as letters. Thus ə ɔ, for example, do not depart very much from the traditions of the roman alphabet, and they fit in well with normal letters; but β ɾ ʅ depart considerably more—they are clearly more exotic shapes than the former, and look more strange beside ordinary letters.

The conventions and traditions of the IPA often allow, for the representation of a particular sound, a choice between two or more different letters. In these cases where such a choice exists, one of the letters will usually be found to be more romanic, in the sense described above, than the alternative (or alternatives). Such ranking of letters according to how relatively romanic they are in shape is, of course, arbitrary, in so far as it must ultimately be a matter of taste; however, when it comes to the point there is usually no doubt. Thus for the vowel in the English word *not* it is, by custom, permitted to use either the letter o, or the letter ɔ,

[1] The use of the word in this convenient sense is due to Daniel Jones.

18

or the letter ɒ. The first symbol is obviously more romanic than
the second, and most people would agree that the second is more
romanic than the third.

To sum up: if, in a transcription of a language, the letters of
most romanic shape have been selected in every case where IPA
conventions allow a choice, then the transcription is said to be
'simple'.

Whether it should also be called 'phonemic' will appear by
examining it in the light of the following principle:

*A simple phonemic transcription uses the smallest possible
number of different letters.* This principle, it will at once be
apparent, is a linguistic one. The smallest possible number of
different letters is the minimum number which suffices to distinguish unambiguously all words of different sound in the language. If less than this minimum were to be employed, then
some words which sound differently would appear in the transcription in identical form. In any transcription of English, for
example, different letters must be found for the consonants
which begin the words *then* and *thin*, or for the vowels in the
words *but* and *put*. This principle does not mean, however, that
we must have one letter for each sound: it means we must have
one for each '*distinctive* sound'. There will, obviously, be many
more different sounds than letters in a phonemic transcription
when it is read aloud. All this comes to the same thing as saying
that there must be one symbol for each *phoneme*, no more and
no less, which is why a transcription made in accordance with
this principle is called 'phonemic'.

### iv Other types of transcription

The most convenient way of describing the other types of
transcription is in terms of *departures* from either one or the
other of the two principles which are the basis of a simple phonemic transcription.

(1) If all the letters in the transcription are *not* the most
romanic ones available, it is not a simple, but a COMPARATIVE
transcription (it may, or may not, be phonemic as well). Such

would be a transcription of RP which made no use of the letter r, but replaced it by ɹ throughout, writing for example ɹaɒnd ðə ɹʌgɪd ɹɒk instead of raɒnd ðə rʌgɪd rɒk.

The most important thing about a *simple* transcription is that the use of the most romanic letters available makes for maximum legibility and ease of printing, writing, and typewriting. The more exotic letters are less likely to be at the disposal of a printer or to be found on a typewriter, and are usually more awkward to write (they often have to be 'drawn' rather than written), and their shapes, though frequently more complex, are less distinctive at a glance. That is what is meant by saying they are less typographically satisfactory. Clearly, there would be no point in abandoning the advantages of a simple transcription unless some other factor were involved. There *is*, however, another factor, and it is this: the more romanic shapes have, by tradition, acquired a more *general* phonetic value than the exotic shapes which are alternatives to them. Therefore in choosing a more exotic letter, where an alternative offers, we are choosing a phonetically more *specific* letter. For example, f is a more romanic letter than ɸ. f is normally the symbol for a voiceless labiodental fricative, and ɸ for a voiceless bilabial fricative. f, however, is a more *general* symbol than ɸ because it can, on occasion, and without violating the principles of the IPA, be used instead of ɸ (IPA, *Principles*, 1949, p. 12).[1] ɸ is therefore not only more exotic than f, but more *specific*: its range of phonetic values is more limited. Similarly a is a more romanic letter than æ; it is also more general, since by tradition it may cover an 'area' of vowel sounds which is larger than, and includes, the area covered by æ.

It turns out, therefore, that the typographical 'scale', from romanic to exotic, along which letters may be ranged according to their familiarity of shape and typographical adequacy, is also a scale, from general to specific, of the phonetic values of the letters. If the principle of a *simple* transcription—that of using the most romanic letters—is departed from, this is obviously not done in order to use the more exotic letters for their own sake,

[1] See Bibliography at end for the full titles of works referred to.

20

but because these more exotic letters will also be more phonetically specific.

A comparative transcription, then, uses symbols some of which, considered in isolation, are more specific in their reference than those of a simple transcription. (It is explained below that only in isolation is a more exotic letter more specific; as used in a transcribed text, a more romanic letter can be made equally specific by the conventions governing the text's interpretation.) The term 'comparative' is chosen as the antithesis of 'simple' because the only reason for preferring an exotic, and therefore more specific, letter to a romanic letter (and therefore sacrificing the typographical advantages of the latter) should be to facilitate the *comparison* of two forms of speech. The comparison may be explicit, as when two or more dialects of a language are being discussed simultaneously; or it may be implicit, as when English is being taught to a French learner. Without such an object in view, it would be pointless to prefer an exotic letter to a more romanic one—the text should be made as typographically adequate as possible. (It is not, all the same, the *motive* which is the basis of the classification; even if an exotic letter is preferred to a more romanic one for no apparent reason, the transcription would still be classified as 'comparative'. There are unfortunately many examples to be found in print of the pointless use of a comparative transcription.)

Transcriptions may be comparative in different degrees: in some cases only one or two, in others a large number of exotic letters may be preferred to more romanic ones.

(2) If the number of different letters is *more* than the minimum as defined above the transcription will not be a phonemic, but an ALLOPHONIC one (it may at the same time be simple also, or it may equally well be comparative). Some of the phonemes, that is to say, will be represented by more than one different symbol. In other words, certain *allophones* of certain phonemes will be singled out for representation in the transcription—hence the term 'allophonic'. An allophonic transcription would be, for example, one of RP which used the two symbols l and ł for 'clear l' and 'dark l' respectively, instead of the single symbol l

for both, since these two sounds are allophones of the same phoneme.

Transcriptions may be allophonic in different degrees: only one or two allophones, or many, may be given separate symbols.

There are thus two different 'dimensions' in which we can depart from a simple phonemic transcription: by increasing the specificity of the symbols, or by increasing the total number of different symbols. Since these departures are independent of each other and can occur at the same time, we have four general types of transcription of any given language:

SIMPLE PHONEMIC (typographically the most satisfactory);

(SIMPLE) ALLOPHONIC—more than the minimum number of letters, but all of them of the most romanic available shapes;

COMPARATIVE (PHONEMIC)—the minimum number of letters, in some cases exotic shapes being preferred to alternative more romanic ones;

COMPARATIVE ALLOPHONIC—more than the minimum number of letters, and in some cases exotic shapes being preferred.

The second and third types can usually be referred to by the terms 'allophonic' and 'comparative' respectively, omitting the words in brackets, without misunderstandings resulting.

A comparative allophonic transcription would be a transcription of RP in which, for instance, the symbols l and ł are used instead of l alone (making it allophonic); and ɹ used instead of r (making it comparative). Such a transcription is used by G. L. Brook (1935).

## v Text and conventions

The difference between these types of transcription can be fully appreciated only when it is remembered that any transcription, whatever the language, has to be *interpreted*: it must properly be looked on as consisting of two parts, the *text*, and the *conventions* which govern the interpretation of the text. The conventions may be tacit, or they may be expressed formally at the beginning of the text; but the text cannot be adequately interpreted by a reader unless he is familiar with the conventions.

## Text and conventions

The conventions which accompany a transcribed text fall into two groups:

(*a*) Those conventions which give phonetic definitions, wherever necessary, of the value of the symbols. In a transcription of RP which uses the letter r, for example, a convention is necessary to explain that this is a post-alveolar fricative or frictionless continuant. Otherwise it could be interpreted as an alveolar rolled consonant, or as various other sounds.

(*b*) Those conventions which explain the contextual variations of the values of the symbols. A transcription of RP which uses only one l symbol can be properly interpreted only if a convention explains that this symbol represents a 'clear' sound before vowels, but a 'dark' one in other cases.

Part of the information, in other words, is conveyed by the text itself, but part is conveyed by the conventions. The essential point to be borne in mind is this: *every departure from a simple phonemic transcription has the effect of transferring information to the text from the conventions*. It has the effect, that is, of making explicit in the transcribed text *distinctions* between speech sounds which in a simple phonemic transcription are confined to the conventions.

Thus a change from a *simple* to a *comparative* transcription transfers information from group (*a*) of the conventions to the text itself. We may illustrate this by comparing two transcriptions of RP, one of which uses the symbol r accompanied by a convention to the effect that this symbol represents a post-alveolar fricative or frictionless continuant, and the other of which uses the symbol ɹ. When ɹ is used the convention is not called for, because the symbol ɹ gives the same information as the convention. The latter transcription is comparative, the former simple.

The distinctions which are made explicit, in the change from a simple to a comparative transcription, are 'external' distinctions, distinctions between the sounds of the form of speech being transcribed and those of some other dialect, language, or accent. In the example just quoted, a distinction is made explicit in the text between a post-alveolar fricative or frictionless continuant and any other sound which may be represented by r (in, say, a transcription of French, or of Scottish English).

A change from a *phonemic* to an *allophonic* transcription, on the other hand, transfers information from group (*b*) of the conventions to the text. The use of the two symbols l and ł in a transcription of RP gives the same information as the convention accompanying a transcription which uses the one symbol l only, to the effect that this latter symbol represents a 'clear' sound before vowels, but a 'dark' one in other cases. If both symbols are used, the convention is not called for.

The distinctions made explicit, in the change from a phonemic to an allophonic transcription, are 'internal' distinctions, distinctions which occur *within* the form of speech being transcribed —distinctions, that is to say, between members of a phoneme, or any other 'segments' to which separate letters are given.

In other words, internal distinctions are made by increasing the total number of symbols, external distinctions by increasing the specificity of the symbols.

These various types of transcription differ from each other, therefore, not in the *total* amount of information which they convey, but in the *relative* amount of information contained in the text as compared with the conventions. The use to which any given transcription is to be put will determine whether it is an advantage to have any given item of information in the text rather than the conventions, for different purposes demand different distributions of the information (Abercrombie, 1954, p. 234); but taking text and conventions together, all these types of transcription are equally informative. It can be seen, therefore, that it is quite misleading to describe any of these types of transcription as more accurate (or more 'scientific') than any other. When correctly made, they are all equally accurate (Scott, 1941).

**vi Quality and quantity**

Differences in the number of letters and in the shapes of letters, then, give rise to the types of transcription described above. These types are universally applicable. We must now consider, however, some other varieties of transcription which spring from quite other sources of difference and which are applicable to certain English accents (of which RP is one), and certain other languages, only. This variation concerns the representation of vowels, and it is necessary to discuss it in some detail, since here lies one of the main points of difference among the traditional transcriptions of RP. The way it comes about is as follows.

The monophthongs which occur in stressed syllables in RP comprise eleven different vowel sounds, i.e. eleven different *auditory qualities*. It is well known that some of these monophthongs are regularly of longer *duration*, in the same phonetic environment, than others (at least in the pronunciation of a very large number of RP speakers). These eleven monophthongs, in fact, can be divided into a group of six 'short' vowels and a group of five 'long' vowels. In addition to these eleven there is a seventh 'short' vowel which is confined to unstressed syllables (it occurs in the first syllable of *about*, or the second syllable of *cupboard*), and which with many speakers is of still another auditory quality (some speakers give it the same quality as the vowel in *bird*). Either the difference of auditory *quality*, or the difference of duration or *quantity*, may form the basis of the way the RP monophthongs are transcribed.

These alternative ways of transcribing depend on the fact that we can establish, from among the RP monophthongs, a number of *pairs* of vowels such that the members of each pair are of different duration and of different though related sound. Such a pair is formed, for example, by the two vowels in *beat* and *bit*. The vowels in this pair, though they are similar, differ from each other in auditory *quality* (resulting from the fact that the first has a higher tongue-position than the second) and also in *quantity* (the first being of longer duration than the second). We can, if we wish, take the quality difference as the basis of the transcription. We would then select two *different* letters—say i and ɪ— for the two vowels, thus symbolizing the quality difference and leaving the quantity difference to be inferred. The words would be transcribed, on this basis, as bit and bɪt respectively. A type of transcription which treats the vowels in this way may conveniently be called a QUALITATIVE transcription. On the other hand we can take the quantity difference as the basis of the transcription, and use the *same* letter—say i—for the two vowels but adding ː, the 'length-mark', after the first, thus symbolizing the quantity difference and leaving the quality difference to be inferred. The words would then appear as biːt and bit respectively. A type of transcription which adopts this treatment of the vowels may be called a QUANTITATIVE transcription.

We can find five pairs of vowels in RP which are susceptible of these alternative treatments.[1] In addition to the vowels in *bit* and *beat*, there are the pairs of vowels in *not* and *nought*, in *look* and *Luke*, in *bat* and *bath*, and also the pair (not quite on the same footing, one member being confined to unstressed syllables) formed by the vowel of *about* or *cupboard*, and the vowel in *bird*. The alternative treatments of these pairs can be shown as follows:

|  |  | *Qualitative* |  | *Quantitative* |  |
|---|---|---|---|---|---|
| bit | beat | bɪt | bit | bit | biːt |
| not | nought | nɒt | nɔt | nɔt | nɔːt |
| look | Luke | lʊk | luk | luk | luːk |
| bat | bath | bat | bɑθ | bat | baːθ |
| cup*board* | bird | kʌbəd | bɜd | kʌbəd | bəːd |

All five pairs are not always treated in the same way in quantitative transcriptions of RP. For example the difference of quality within a pair is at its greatest in the case of the vowels of *bat* and *bath*. Some transcribers have felt it to be too great a difference for a quantitative treatment of the pair to be justified, and they have therefore not included it with the rest. Other transcribers have preferred not to treat the vowels of *cupboard* and *bird* as a quantitative pair in spite of their closely similar quality, because of the rather special function in the vowel system of RP that the 'short' one has, confined as it is to unstressed syllables. Still other transcribers have excluded from

[1] Other 'pairings' are possible; however, they have seldom been made the basis of transcriptions (Gimson, 1945–9, p. 94).

quantitative treatment the pairs of vowels in *bit* and *beat* and in *look* and *Luke* on the grounds that the vowels of *beat* and *Luke* are not monophthongs but diphthongs, and should be transcribed as such. This interpretation is further discussed below (p. 33).

It would, of course, be redundant to transcribe these RP pairs of vowels in such a way as to indicate at the same time both their quantity and their quality, since the one can always be inferred from the other. Is it, then, a matter of indifference which basis, quantitative or qualitative, is selected for transcribing vowels; or is one basis better than the other in any way? This is not a simple question to answer, and there has in fact been considerable difference of opinion among phoneticians and linguists concerning the respective merits of the two treatments.

An important consideration here is that the adoption of the quantitative basis means that a smaller number of different letters is needed for the vowels than would otherwise be the case (a comparison of the two ways of transcribing the five pairs of words given above on p. 26 shows this quite clearly), and in the opinion of some phoneticians this symbol-economy is a sufficiently good reason for preferring a quantitative transcription to a qualitative one. On the other hand there are phoneticians who claim that this economy is attained only at the expense of misusing the length-mark to indicate sound-quality instead of just duration, and therefore that quantitative transcriptions are to be condemned as linguistically unsound.

Arguments about the legitimacy of this use of the length-mark, and about the respective merits in general of the two treatments of RP vowels, have often been obscured by failure to distinguish between three quite different questions: first, whether the two treatments are equally well-founded phonemically; second, whether they indicate with equal fidelity the factors on which recognition by the listener of spoken words depends; and third, whether they are equally suitable for language-teaching purposes. These three questions must be kept separate in any discussion of the merits of quantitative and qualitative transcriptions of RP.

It can be claimed that both treatments represent equally justifiable phonemic analyses, though they result in a different inventory of phonemes: in a qualitative transcription each different vowel quality is considered to belong to a different phoneme, whereas in a quantitative transcription some of the different vowel qualities are considered to be determined by the phonetic environments in which they occur, and therefore in those cases not to constitute separate phonemes.

In this latter view, the different vowel qualities in the words *bit* and *beat* are comparable to the different consonant qualities which begin the words *key* and *car*. These two different consonant qualities are not considered to be separate phonemes, because they are determined by the different environments in which they occur, that is to say by the different vowels which follow them. It might at first seem as if in *bit* and *beat* the environments of the vowels were identical. Each has the same consonant before it and the same consonant after it, and the environment of both of them would thus appear to be b . . t. However, the environments are in fact different from each other in one very important respect: the b and the t are more widely separated from each other in the second word than in the first, and the vowel in the second word therefore has a bigger gap to fill. The environment of the first vowel, certainly, is

b . . t

but that of the second is really

b . . . t

Thus when the words *bit* and *beat* are transcribed bit and biːt respectively, the function of the length-mark as used in the second word is, in this view, to indicate the difference of environment of its vowel, as compared with that of the first word. The difference of quality between the two vowels is always tied to this difference of environment, and the two qualities are not considered to be distinct phonemes, but to be allophones of the same phoneme determined by their environment. Therefore if the transcription is phonemic, and not allophonic, the vowels will receive the same symbol, i—just as in a phonemic transcrip-

28

tion the initial consonants of *key* and *car* are both transcribed k. In both cases the context of the symbol is enough to indicate the quality of the sound to which it refers. The same reasoning applies to the quantitative treatment of the other pairs of vowels (Jones, 1950, Ch. XXIII).

We must conclude, then, that qualitative and quantitative transcriptions represent equally legitimate phonemic analyses of RP vowels. There can be little doubt, however, that the listener's ability to discriminate between the words *bit* and *beat* depends on the sound-quality, not the duration, of their vowels, and the same is true of the other pairs.[1] This fact of perception is reflected, of course, in qualitative transcriptions but not in quantitative ones, and here therefore the two sorts of transcription are not equal, though many would hold that this is not a very important consideration. Certainly people who prefer to use a quantitative transcription do not do so because they wrongly believe discrimination between *bit* and *beat* to depend on vowel duration; the fact that it does not do so they hold to be irrelevant.

If discrimination between spoken words such as *bit* and *beat* depends on the sound-quality of their vowels, then the foreign learner who wishes his spoken English to be intelligible must be capable of making this qualitative distinction. It does not follow, however, that he will be helped to acquire this and the other similar distinctions, if he does not already possess them, by being taught to speak by the help of a qualitative transcription. A number of experienced teachers of English pronunciation, and notably Daniel Jones and P. A. D. MacCarthy (1956*b*), have emphasized this point. Phonetic symbols cannot in themselves

[1] Various experiments have fairly conclusively demonstrated the paramount importance of vowel quality for recognition (Gimson, 1945–9). Words are still recognizable if the length of their vowels is distorted but the quality is kept unchanged, whereas the reverse is not the case.

It should not be forgotten, moreover, that a (probably increasing) number of RP speakers do not make the quantitative difference in their speech; yet this does not affect their intelligibility, and is certainly not even detected by the average listener. (The 'quantitative' analysis is, of course, inapplicable to these speakers.) The qualitative difference is always there; the quantitative one may or may not be, and is to this extent less essential.

teach pronunciation: sounds have to be taught quite independently of symbols, the only purpose of which is to identify unambiguously the sounds once they have been learnt. Indeed, the less the number of different phonetic symbols the average language learner has to cope with, the better. The maximum symbol economy is afforded by a quantitative transcription which is also a simple phonemic one (see Specimens I and II in Appendix I). Texts transcribed in this style are extremely legible, and well suited to learners who simply wish to acquire English and do not intend to become specialist phoneticians. Such transcriptions, moreover, have the advantage for the teacher that he has to overcome less resistance on the part of his pupils to phonetic notation. (Hostility to exotic letters, particularly when used in conjunction with the normal letters of the roman alphabet, seems to be almost universal, even among people whose mother-tongue is not written in the roman alphabet.)

There are, however, other pedagogical uses of phonetic transcription, as well as those connected with foreign-language teaching: it is a necessity, for instance, for native English speakers who are studying the phonetics of their own language. Although symbol-economy is an important consideration in teaching English pronunciation for purely practical ends, for teaching the phonetics of English, in the full sense, it is hardly important at all. In fact types of transcription in which a quantitative treatment is avoided are of great advantage here, for it must be remembered that other elements in RP, besides vowels, have quantitative aspects. The length of syllables is particularly important in connexion with a number of problems, and the length of consonants must also sometimes be taken into consideration. A qualitative transcription, where there is *no* indication of quantity, makes it much easier to discuss all aspects of quantity impartially.

Although, as was mentioned above, it may be redundant to indicate both quantity and quality in a transcription of RP, it may nevertheless be useful at times to do so; see, for example, Specimen V in Appendix I, p. 85. A transcription of this sort, writing bɪt biːt, nɒt nɔːt, and so on, using different symbols *and* a length-mark in each pair of vowels, is best classified as quantitative and allophonic: special symbols are allotted to allophones of vowels, thereby making explicit in the text an 'internal' distinction which otherwise would be dealt with by a convention explaining the environments in which the two vowel qualities are used.

Both quantitative and qualitative transcriptions can be combined with all the characteristics of phonemic or allophonic, and simple or comparative, transcriptions, so that a number of varieties of both are possible.

### vii Phonemic interpretation and diphthongs

The quantitative and qualitative types of transcription which have just been described have their origin, as we have seen, in a difference of *phonemic interpretation* of the 'raw material' which is to be transcribed. The possibility of such differences in the reduction of the sounds of a language to a system of phonemes arises moderately frequently (Chao, 1933), and another point in English where there can be divergence of this sort, this time concerning consonants, is exemplified by the part of the word *chew* that comes before the vowel. According to some analyses of English this part consists of two consonant phonemes, while according to other analyses it consists of only one consonant phoneme. These different views, naturally, will probably be reflected in transcription: if the consonantal beginning of the word is regarded as two phonemes, it is very likely to be transcribed with two letters, for instance tʃ, whereas if it is regarded as one phoneme it is more likely to be transcribed with only one, perhaps either the ligature tʃ, or the symbol c (IPA, *Principles*, 1949, p. 15). The consonantal beginning of the word *jaw* affords an exactly parallel case.[1]

These are relatively minor instances of difference in phonemic interpretation, as far as consequences for transcription go. More

[1] Daniel Jones, however, who regards the consonantal parts of these two words as each consisting of a single phoneme, nevertheless transcribes them with two separate letters.

far-reaching consequences arise in connexion with differing phonemic interpretations of the RP diphthongs, about which something must now be said.

Transcriptions of RP made according to IPA principles customarily use two letters for transcribing a diphthong: the first letter indicates the starting-point, or first 'element', and the second letter indicates the ending-point, or second 'element', of the diphthong.[1] No new letters need be introduced into the transcription for the elements of diphthongs (though some transcribers have done so; see below): the two letters can be chosen from among those already needed by the transcription for other purposes. There may however be more than one possible choice, both for the first element and for the second. For example, the first element of the diphthong in the word *eye* may be allotted either the same letter as the one used for the vowel in *bad*, or as the one used for the vowel in *bath*, or as the one used for the vowel in *bud*. It is not identical with any of these three (though they are the nearest to it in sound-quality), and there seems to be no cogent reason for preferring one of them to any of the others; indeed all three representations of the diphthong can be found in published texts. The choice, however, is in effect a phonemic decision; in making it the first element is identified, explicitly or implicitly, with the phoneme to which the monophthong, whose symbol is preferred, belongs.

The same possibility of different phonemic interpretations exists for the first element of the diphthongs in the word *now*, and there are also alternative choices for the first elements of the diphthongs in *no* (the vowel in *board* or the vowel in *bird*), *boy* (the vowel in *bog* or the vowel in *board*, and *there* (the vowel in *bed* or the vowel in *bad*), and all these interpretations can be found in published texts. Some of them are further discussed in Appendix I. All are possible because in no case does the sound-quality of the first element coincide exactly with the sound-quality of any of the monophthongs.

[1] There have in the past been systems of transcription of English in which diphthongs have been given single symbols, but none appear to be in use now.

# Phonemic interpretation and diphthongs

The second element of RP diphthongs also offers opportunities for comparable differences in phonemic interpretation. In the diphthongs in the words *day*, *eye* and *boy* the second element (which is the same in all three) may be identified either with the vowel in the word *bid*, and transcribed as i or ɪ; or it may be identified with the consonant at the beginning of the word *you*, and transcribed j. Similarly, in the diphthongs in the words *no* and *now* the second element (which is the same in both) may be identified either with the vowel in the word *good*, and transcribed u or ɷ; or it may be identified with the consonant at the beginning of the word *we*, and transcribed w. We may call it a *vocalic* treatment of the second element if it is identified with the vowel of *bid* or of *good*, and a *consonantal* treatment of the second element if it is identified with the consonant of *you* or of *we*. A vocalic treatment is perhaps the more common of the two, but it is worth recalling that the consonantal treatment has a long history, dating from well before the founding of the IPA, and going back at least to Thomas Batchelor (1809).

Most of the transcribers who have adopted a consonantal treatment of the second element of these five diphthongs have extended the treatment to the vowels of the words *bead* and *food*, regarding them as diphthongs rather than monophthongs, and accordingly transcribing the words as bijd, fuwd (Batchelor was one of the first to do this). Some transcribers have adopted the consonantal treatment for these two vowels only, the rest of the diphthongs receiving a vocalic treatment; see, for example, Henry Sweet's English text in the IPA *Exposé des Principes* (1900).

The second element common to the remaining diphthongs, those in the words *here*, *there* and *poor*, has nearly always been transcribed in accordance with a vocalic treatment as ə, being identified with the vowel at the beginning of the word *again*. An alternative treatment, a consonantal one, has however gained some acceptance during the last twenty years (Trager and Bloch, 1941). In this case the second element is identified with the consonant at the beginning of the word *heard* and is accordingly transcribed h, even though the two are fairly far removed from each other in sound-quality, one being voiced and the other being voiceless. A consonantal treatment of all diphthongs is illustrated in Appendix I, Specimen VIII.

By choice of letter, therefore, we may in a transcription identify an element of a diphthong with one of the monophthongs (or, if it is the second element, one of the consonants), though the sound-qualities of the two do not exactly coincide. In such cases, the text of the transcription needs to be accompanied by a convention to the effect that in the context of the diphthong the symbol is to be interpreted differently from elsewhere. If, however, we choose a special letter, having no other function in the transcription, for an element of a diphthong, the existence of a difference of sound-quality is thereby made explicit in the text— we have drawn an 'internal' distinction. In transcriptions of RP diphthongs either the first or the second element may be represented in this way, by a letter having no other function. For example, a transcription may use æ in *bad*, ɑ in *bath*, and ʌ in *bud*, but introduce a fourth letter, say a, for the first element of the diphthong in *eye*.

It is less common to find this sort of thing arising in connexion with the second element of RP diphthongs. An example, however, is the use of special letters, having no other function, to represent the second element of the vowels in *bead*, *food*, when these are treated as diphthongs (see above, p. 33). Transcriptions have been published in which the first elements are given the same letters, ɪ, ɷ, as are used for the monophthongs in the words *bit*, *put*, and the second elements the letters i, u, which are used only in these two combinations and nowhere else in the transcription; the diphthongs thus appear as ɪi, ɷu, respectively.

When special letters are used in a transcription for the first or the second elements of diphthongs, the transcription is to be classified as an allophonic one, in so far as 'internal' distinctions are made explicit in the text (although some theories concerning the phonemic status of the 'elements' of diphthongs might seem to make this application of the term inappropriate).[1]

---

[1] Daniel Jones, who considers the diphthongs of RP to be single phonemes, has introduced a special extra category of transcriptions ('multi-

## viii 'Broad' and 'narrow'

The terms 'broad' and 'narrow' have been used as labels for types of phonetic transcription for the last fifty years, but unfortunately they have developed a number of different meanings. Henry Sweet, with whom the terms originated, used them chiefly as equivalents of what I have called *simple* and *comparative* respectively. However, as early as 1911 (Sčerba) they had come to be used as equivalents of *phonemic* and *allophonic* respectively, and this is probably now their commonest sense, although the earlier sense still persists: the terms are used in both ways, for example, in the current (1949) edition of the IPA *Principles*. In putting forward the more precisely defined labels explained in this Introduction, I am not suggesting that the older labels 'broad' and 'narrow' should be dispensed with. They remain useful for occasions when precision is not required, and it is then convenient to use 'broad' as an equivalent of *simple phonemic*, and 'narrow' for any departure from this, either in the direction of *comparative* or in the direction of *allophonic*, or both together.

A third use that the terms are sometimes put to in discussion of RP transcriptions is to apply 'broad' to a transcription based on a quantitative treatment of the monophthongs, and 'narrow' to a transcription based on a qualitative treatment (see, e.g., Enkvist, 1955). This further extension of the meaning of the terms unnecessarily increases the confusion and, although it has become fairly common, it would be a good thing if it could be discontinued.

All the types of transcription which have been discussed in the foregoing pages belong to a general category which I have elsewhere (1953) called *systematic* transcriptions, as opposed to another category of *impressionistic* (or non-systematic) transcriptions. In the latter type the elements, or segments, of utterances are symbolized by being referred to *general phonetic* categories rather than, as is the case with the types of transcription

literal') to deal with this point (see *Outline of English Phonetics*, 8th edition, p. 336).

we have here been considering, to sound-systems of given languages. Impressionistic transcriptions are used for certain specialized purposes. They are often attempts to portray unique utterances, or parts of utterances, which are not 'systematizable', such as defective speech, infant noises, and so on. Impressionistic transcriptions are also necessarily used on occasions when a sound-system has not yet been established, as in field-work on dialects or unknown languages. The terms 'broad' and 'narrow' have been used as synonyms of *systematic* and *impressionistic* respectively, giving yet a fourth sense for them to bear; but it would seem best to discontinue this usage also.

## ix Characteristics of the present transcription

The type of transcription used in the following texts, sometimes known as 'Edinburgh' transcription, would traditionally be called 'narrow' for more than one of the reasons given above. In our terminology it would be described as *simple*; *allophonic* as regards the first elements of the diphthongs eɪ, oʊ, though phonemic in other respects; *qualitative* in its representation of monophthongs; *vocalic* in its treatment of second elements of diphthongs. It will be noted that the transcription uses a total number of fourteen different vowel letters, viz.: a e i o u ɐ ɒ ɔ ɛ ə ɪ ɔ ʊ ʌ. The symbol æ does not appear among them.

A transcription which avoids length-marks has been preferred for the present purpose to a quantitative one, for the reasons explained above (p. 30): the texts are primarily intended for use by students, either native English-speaking or foreign, whose interest is in English phonetics and phonology rather than in learning English pronunciation. They will therefore need to pay attention to other aspects of quantity in addition to that of vowels.

The use of æ in IPA transcriptions of RP goes back to the time when phonetic texts in English were intended almost entirely for teaching pronunciation to French and German learners of the language, and because of this it was thought necessary to draw special attention to the difference in quality between the vowel in English *pat* and the vowel in French *patte* by using a distinctive letter for the former. The force of tradition has been strong enough to perpetuate this use of æ even in transcribed texts where there is no particular reason to emphasize the difference. There is certainly no reason to do so as far as the present texts are concerned. In any case this vowel in RP seems to be becoming both less front and also more open (a tendency which may also be observed in some types of Cockney accent)—in other words the vowel is losing the characteristics which originally singled it out for special attention. (It is noteworthy that Daniel Jones has dropped the symbol æ in recent—the third and fourth—editions of his *Pronunciation of English*.)

The allophonic representation of the first elements of the diphthongs in the words *date* and *note*, which are transcribed as deɪt and noʊt (the letters e and o not being used elsewhere for vowels) is made necessary by the circumstances in which the transcription is likely to be used, that is to say with groups of students in which other accents of English, as well as RP, are spoken and transcribed. In the early stages of teaching it is important that students should not be confused by apparent conflict between transcriptions of these different accents. For example, in educated Scots the vowels in the two words *debt* and *date*, say, must be transcribed dɛt and det (since the second word contains a monophthong). It is best, therefore, to transcribe the RP pronunciation of these two words as dɛt and deɪt, rather than, for instance, det and deɪt: this, though it avoids being allophonic, would inevitably give rise to confusion since det would then represent *debt* in one accent and *date* in the other. The same considerations apply to the vowels in *nought* and *note*, which in educated Scots have to be transcribed nɔt and not, thereby ruling out the use for transcribing RP at the same time of not and noʊt respectively.

The present type of transcription is closely related to, indeed is ultimately based on, the type exhibited in Specimen V, Appendix I (p. 85). The latter is different only in preserving the letter æ, and in using length-marks to distinguish some of the allophones of vowels which vary in duration from others. Very similar (though not identical) types of transcription, all of which avoid length-marks and would also be called 'narrow', have appeared in C. F. Mackenzie and P. W. Drew's *Phonetic Reader* (1919) and Dorothée Palmer's annotated phonetic edition of *The Mollusc* by H. H. Davies (1938), and have been used from time to time by contributors to *Le Maître Phonétique* from 1926 until the present day (among them Daniel Jones, Lilias Armstrong, H. E. Palmer, E. Kruisinga, A. C. Lawrenson, R. Grant Brown, A. C. Pring, K. H. Albrow). The fact that there is a need for such a type of transcription was pointed out in the IPA *Principles* (1912), p. 20, and a specimen text is given there in illustration.

## x  The transcribed texts

In view of the probable interests of students who will be using this book, passages have been chosen for transcription which in themselves have some relevance to linguistic studies (some of the passages, indeed, might provide topics for class discussion). Two of them, numbers 15 and 16, have been included because they have so often been used for phonetic texts before. The former passage, 'The Story of Arthur the Rat', has also been widely used for collecting sound-recordings of different accents and dialects of English. The original version of the text first appeared, as far as I am aware, in 1890 in Henry Sweet's *A Primer of Spoken English* (the rat was then called Grip), and the story seems to have been composed by Sweet. It is nowadays current in a number of different versions, all shorter than the original, and all modified in various places in order to cover as many of the phonetic and phonological points of variation of the English-speaking world as possible. It is these shorter versions that have been used by various institutions for making collections of recordings; for instance, by Columbia University from the 1930's onwards, and by Edinburgh University since 1950. The version given here is the one modified for use in Edinburgh. The other text, 'The North Wind and the Sun', has traditionally been used in publications of the IPA for providing specimen transcriptions of different kinds of English, and, in translation, specimens of other languages.

The text composed by H. E. Palmer (number 17) is a very convenient one for illustrating economically different types of transcription, and it has been used for this purpose in Appendix I.

The style of delivery which is represented here is, to use J. D. O'Connor's term (1948), 'formal colloquial'. This is in keeping with the nature of the transcribed texts.

# Part II

---

## TEXTS

# NOTE

Alternative pronunciations of words have not been indicated.

A number of words ending in *-less*, *-ness*, *-ate* are shown as having the vowel ə in these endings, where many speakers would use ɪ.

An asterisk * is prefixed to the transcribed versions of all names of people and places on their first appearance.

For reasons of legibility, sans serif type is not used for the connected phonetic texts.

# 1. ˈlaŋgwɪdʒ

ˈlaŋgwɪdʒ—ˈhjumən ˈspitʃ—ɪz ən ɪnɪgˈzɔstəbl̩ əˈbʌndəns əv
ˈmanɪfoʊld ˈtrɛʒəz. ˈlaŋgwɪdʒ ɪz ɪnˈsɛprəbl̩ frəm ˈman ən ˈfɒloʊz
hɪm ɪn ˈɔl hɪz ˈwɜks. ˈlaŋgwɪdʒ ɪz ði ˈɪnstrʊmənt wɪð wɪtʃ ˈman
ˈfɔmz ˈθɔt ən ˈfilɪŋ, ˈmud, aspɪˈreɪʃn̩, ˈwɪl ənd ˈakt, ði ˈɪnstrʊmənt
baɪ huz ˈminz hi ˈɪnflʊənsɪz ənd ɪz ˈɪnflʊənst, ði ˈʌltɪmət, ən
ˈdipɪst faʊnˈdeɪʃn̩ əv ˈhjumən səˈsaɪətɪ. bət ɪt ɪz ˈɔlsoʊ ði ˈʌltɪmət,
ɪndɪsˈpɛnsəbl̩ səsˈteɪnər əv ðə ˈhjumən ɪndɪˈvɪdʒʊəl, hɪz ˈrɛfjudʒ
ɪn ˈaʊəz əv ˈloʊnlɪnəs, wɛn ðə ˈmaɪnd ˈrɛslz wɪð ɪgˈzɪstəns ən ðə
ˈkɒnflɪkt ɪz rɪˈzɒlvd ɪn ðə ˈmɒnəlɒg əv ðə ˈpoʊɪt ən ðə ˈθɪŋkə.
bɪˈfɔ ðə ˈfɜst əˈweɪknɪŋ əv aʊə ˈkɒnʃəsnəs ˈlaŋgwɪdʒ wəz ˈɛkoʊɪŋ
əˈbaʊt əs, ˈrɛdɪ tə ˈkloʊz əˈraʊnd aʊə ˈfɜst ˈtɛndə ˈsid əv ˈθɔt ən
tʊ əˈkʌmpənɪ əs ɪnˈsɛprəblɪ θru ˈlaɪf, frəm ðə ˈsɪmpl akˈtɪvətɪz əv
ˈɛvrɪdeɪ ˈlɪvɪŋ tʊ aʊə moʊst səˈblaɪm ənd ˈɪntɪmət ˈmoʊmənts—
ˈðoʊz ˈmoʊmənts frəm wɪtʃ wi ˈbɒroʊ ˈwɔmθ ən ˈstrɛŋθ fər aʊə
ˈdeɪlɪ ˈlaɪf θru ðat ˈhoʊld əv ˈmɛmərɪ ðət ˈlaŋgwɪdʒ ɪtˈsɛlf ˈgɪvz
əs. bət ˈlaŋgwɪdʒ ɪz ˈnoʊ ɪksˈtɜnl̩ əˈkʌmpənɪmənt. ɪt laɪz ˈdip ɪn
ðə ˈmaɪnd əv ˈman, ə ˈwɛlθ əv ˈmɛmərɪz ɪnˈhɛrɪtɪd baɪ ði ɪndɪˈvɪdʒʊəl ən ðə ˈtraɪb, ə ˈvɪdʒɪlənt ˈkɒnʃəns ðət rɪˈmaɪndz ənd ˈwɔnz.
ən ˈspitʃ ɪz ðə dɪsˈtɪŋtɪv ˈmak əv ðə pɜsn̩ˈalətɪ, fə ˈgʊd ənd ˈɪl,
ðə dɪsˈtɪŋtɪv ˈmak əv ˈhoʊm ənd əv ˈneɪʃn̩, man'kaɪndz ˈpeɪtn̩t əv
noʊˈbɪlətɪ. soʊ ɪnˈɛkstrɪkəblɪ həz ˈlaŋgwɪdʒ ˈgroʊn ɪnsaɪd pɜsn̩-
ˈalətɪ, ˈhoʊm, ˈneɪʃn̩, man'kaɪnd, ən ˈlaɪf ɪtˈsɛlf ðət wi meɪ
ˈsʌmtaɪmz bɪ ˈtɛmptɪd tʊ ˈask wɛðə ˈlaŋgwɪdʒ ɪz ə ˈmɪə rɪˈflɛkʃən
ɒv, ə ˈsɪmplɪ ˈɪz nɒt ˈɔl ðoʊz ˈθɪŋz—ðə ˈvɛrɪ ˈsid ˈlif əv ðɛə ˈgroʊθ.

Louis Hjelmslev, 1943, translated by Francis J. Whitfield

43

## 2. kən'troʊl əv 'laŋgwɪdʒ

əˈparəntlı wi səˈpoʊz ðət ðə "gɪft' əv ˈlaŋgwɪdʒ ɪz laık ðə "gɪft' əv ə ˈnoʊz, ɪnˈtaıəlı (əz tʊ ɪts pəˈzıʃn̩ ənd ˈɒfıs) aʊtˈsaıd ðə ˈskoʊp əv aʊə ˈmɒdıfaıɪŋ kənˈtroʊl. ənd ɪt s ˈtru ðət wi ˈkanɒt ɪnˈvɜt aʊə noʊz, ə ˈgıv ɪt ˈfə ˈnɒstrəlz, ə prıˈzɛnt ɪt wıð ðə ˈpaʊər əv ˈhıərıŋ ə ˈsaıt. ˈnaıðər, ɪndid, kən wi dıˈvɛləp ɪt ɪntʊ ən ˈɔgən əv (ət ˈprɛzn̩t) tranˈsɛndənt smɛl, ˈnoʊ, nər ˈivn̩ rısˈtə tʊ ɪt ɪts ˈprıstin ən ˈsʌbˈhjumən ˈprıvəlıdʒız. bət ˈəl ðıs ˈoʊnlı ˈʃoʊz ðət wi həd ˈbɛtə ˈliv ɒf ˈtɔkıŋ əv "gɪft' wɛn ˈspikıŋ əv ˈlaŋgwɪdʒ. ˈraðə, wi həv ˈpeınfəlı ˈɪnd ðə pəˈzɛʃn̩ əv ˈspıtʃ baı ˈlɜnıŋ tə kənˈtroʊl ən ˈɔdə ðə ˈsaʊndz prəˈdjusəbl̩ baı aʊər ıˈvɒlvıŋ ˈlarıŋks, ən baı kənˈtınjoʊəslı, kənˈsıstəntlı, ˈadjoʊəslı, ˈpəpəsıvlı dıˈvɛləpıŋ ðə kəmˈplɛksətız əv ðə rıˈzʌltıŋ ˈsıstəm əv ˈvoʊkl̩ ˈsaınz. ɪn ˈduıŋ ðıs wi həv ıˈvɒlvd ən dıˈvɛləpt ˈsıntaks ən ˈprɒsədı ən ˈmʌtʃ ˈɛls ðət ðə fıˈlɒlədʒıst, ˈɒrətə, ə ˈpoʊıt kən ıksˈpaʊnd tʊ əs, ə ˈjuz tə ˈınfloʊəns aʊə ˈfilıŋ ən ˈakʃən. ðə ˈpɒınt ˈız, ðət ˈdʒʌst wɛn ðə ˈnid əv ˈadıŋ kənˈsɛnsəs tʊ ə ˈsoʊ far əˈkʌmplıʃt kənˈtroʊl wəz ˈmoʊst ˈɜdʒənt, ənd ıts nıˈglɛkt ˈmoʊst ˈsɜtn̩ tə bi dıˈzastrəs tə aʊər ıntəˈlɛktʃoʊəl ˈfɒtʃunz; ˈdʒʌst wɛn ə ˈhaı sıvəlaıˈzeıʃn̩ ən ˈwɒt wi ˈkəl ðə ˈmɒdn̩ ˈıərə əv dısˈkʌvərı ənd ɪts riˈakʃən ɒn fıləˈsɒfıkl̩ ˈθɒt ən ˈpraktıkl̩ ˈlaıf sɛts ˈın, wi bıˈgan tə ˈluz ˈmɔr ən ˈmɔ ðə ˈvɛrı aıˈdıə əv ə ˈsoʊʃl̩ kənˈtroʊl, ənd əv ˈpaʊə tə dəˈrɛkt ðə dıˈvɛləpmənt, əv ðə moʊst ˈprɛʃəs əv ˈəl aʊə rıˈkwaıəmənts, ðat əv ɑˈtıkjələt ˈspıtʃ.

aı kən ˈnɛvə fəˈgɛt ði əˈmeızmənt aı ˈfɛlt wɛn aı ˈfɜst bıˈgan maı ˈstʌdı əv fıˈlɒlədʒı, ən ˈrıəlaızd ðıs ˈfakt ənd ıts ˈfʊl sıgˈnıfıkəns. ðə ˈraıtəz ˈwʌn ən ˈəl ˈtritıd ˈlaŋgwɪdʒ, ˈnɒt əz ju wəd ˈtrit ˈmʌsl̩, əz ə ˈminz əv ˈwɜk tə bı ˈbrɔt ʌndə ðə ˈmoʊst maınˈjut, ıˈlabərət ən ʌnˈfeılıŋ ˈfʌŋkʃənl̩ kənˈtroʊl, bət əz ju maıt ˈtrit sʌm ˈdıstənt

44

kɒnstə'leɪʃn̩ ɪn 'speɪs ənd ɪts, tɔ 'ʌs, mɪs'tɪərɪəs 'muvmənts. ɪt 'dʌznt 'sim tɔ əv 'dənd əpɒn 'ɛnɪ wʌn, aɪðə 'spɛʃlɪst ə "leɪ', wɒt ə trɪ'mɛndəs əb'sɜdətɪ 'ðɪs 'weɪ əv rɪ'gɑdɪŋ 'laŋgwɪdʒ ɪn'vɒlvz.

LADY WELBY, 1911

## 3. 'proɒz, 'vɜs ənd 'spitʃ

'wɛðə wi juz 'proɒz ə 'vɜs ɒn ðə 'steɪdʒ, ðeɪ ə 'boɒθ bət 'minz tɒ ən 'ɛnd. ðə 'dɪfrəns, frəm 'wʌn pɔɪnt əv vju, ɪz 'nɒt soɒ 'greɪt əz wi maɪt 'θɪŋk. ɪn 'ðoɒz 'proɒz 'pleɪz wɪtʃ sə'vaɪv, wɪtʃ ə 'rɛd ņ prə'djust ɒn ðə 'steɪdʒ baɪ 'leɪtə dʒɛnə'reɪʃņz, ðə 'proɒz ɪn wɪtʃ ðə 'karɪktəz 'spik ɪz əz rɪ'moɒt, fə ðə 'bɛst pat, frəm ðə və'kabjələrɪ, 'sɪntaks ən 'rɪðəm əv aɒər 'ɔdņrɪ spitʃ—wɪð ɪts 'fʌmblɪŋ fə 'wɜdz, ɪts 'kɒnstənt rɪ'kɔs tɒ əprɒksɪ'meɪʃņ, ɪts dɪs'ɔdə ənd ɪts ʌn'fɪnɪʃt 'sɛntənsɪz—əz 'vɜs ɪz. 'laɪk vɜs, ɪt həz bɪn 'rɪtņ, ənd 'rɪrɪtņ. aɒə 'tu 'greɪtɪst 'proɒz 'staɪlɪsts ɪn ðə 'drɑmə—ə'pɑt frəm *'ʃeɪkspɪər ən ði 'ʌðər ɪlɪzə'biθŋz hu 'mɪkst 'proɒz ən 'vɜs ɪn ðə 'seɪm 'pleɪ—'ɑr, aɪ bəliv, *'kɒŋgriv ən *'bɜnəd *'ʃɔ. ə 'spitʃ baɪ ə 'karɪktər əv 'kɒŋgriv ɔr əv 'ʃɔ 'haz—haɒ'ɛvə 'klɪəlɪ ðə 'karɪktəz meɪ bɪ dɪfə'rɛnʃɪeɪtɪd—ðat ʌnmis'teɪkəbļ 'pɜsņļ 'rɪðəm wɪtʃ 'oɒnlɪ ðə moɒst ə'kʌmplɪʃt kɒnvə'seɪʃņļɪsts—hu 'ɑ fə 'ðat matə 'juʒəlɪ mɒn'ɒlədʒɪsts—ʃoɒ 'ɛnɪ 'treɪs ɪn ðɛə 'tɔk. wi əv 'ɔl 'hɜd ('tu 'ɒfņ!) əv *'mɒlɪɛəz 'karɪktə hu ɪks'prɛst sə'praɪz wɛn 'toɒld ðət i 'spoɒk 'proɒz. bət ɪt wəz *'məsjə *ʒur'dɛ̃ hu wəz 'raɪt, ən 'nɒt hɪz 'mɛntər ə kri'eɪtə: hi dɪd 'nɒt spik 'proɒz—hi oɒnlɪ 'tɔkt. fər aɪ 'min tə 'drɔ ə 'trɪpļ dɪs'tɪŋkʃən: bɪtwin 'proɒz, ən 'vɜs, ənd aɒər 'ɔdņrɪ spitʃ wɪtʃ ɪz 'moɒstlɪ bɪ'loɒ ðə 'lɛvļ əv aɪðə 'vɜs 'ɔ 'proɒz. soɒ ɪf ju 'lɒk ət ɪt ɪn 'ðɪs weɪ, ɪt wɪl ə'pɪə ðət 'proɒz, ɒn ðə 'steɪdʒ, ɪz əz ɑtɪ'fɪʃļ əz 'vɜs: ɔr ɒl'tɜnətɪvlɪ, ðət 'vɜs kən bi əz 'natʃrəl əz 'proɒz.

T. S. Eliot, 1950

46

## 4. 'fatɪk kə'mjunjən

ə 'mɪə 'freɪz əv pə'laɪtnəs, ɪn 'jus əz 'mʌtʃ əmʌŋ 'savɪdʒ 'traɪbz əz ɪn ə 'jʊərəpɪən 'drɔɪŋ-rʊm, fʊl'fɪlz ə 'fʌŋkʃən tə wɪtʃ ðə 'minɪŋ əv ɪts 'wɜdz ɪz 'ɔlmoʊst kəm'plɪtlɪ ɪ'rɛləvənt. ɪŋ'kwaɪərɪz əbaʊt 'hɛlθ, 'kɒmɛnts ɒn 'wɛðə, afə'meɪʃn̩z əv sʌm sʊ'primlɪ 'ɒbvɪəs 'steɪt əv θɪŋz—'ɔl 'sʌtʃ ər ɪks'tʃeɪnʒd, 'nɒt ɪn ədə tʊ ɪn'fɔm, 'nɒt ɪn 'ðɪs keɪs tə kə'nɛkt pipl ɪn 'akʃən, 'sɜtn̩lɪ nɒt ɪn 'ədə tʊ ɪks'prɛs ɛnɪ 'θɔt. ɪt wʊd bɪ 'ivn̩ ɪŋkə'rɛkt, aɪ 'θɪŋk, tə 'seɪ ðət 'sʌtʃ 'wɜdz 'sɜv ðə 'pɜpəs əv ɪs'tablɪʃɪŋ ə 'kɒmən 'sɛntɪmənt, fə ðɪs ɪz 'juʒəlɪ 'absənt frəm sʌtʃ 'kʌrənt 'freɪzɪz əv 'intəkəs; ən wɛər ɪt 'pɜpəts tə ɪg'zɪst, əz ɪn ɪk'spreʃn̩z əv 'sɪmpəθɪ, ɪt ɪz ə'vaʊɪdlɪ 'spjʊərɪəs ɒn 'wʌn saɪd. 'wɒt ɪz ðə 'reɪzɒn 'dɛtr, ðɛəfɔr, əv 'sʌtʃ 'freɪzɪz əz 'haʊ d jʊ 'du?' ''ɑ, 'hɪə ju ɑ,' ''wɛə d jʊ 'kʌm frɒm?' ''naɪs 'deɪ tədeɪ' —'ɔl əv wɪtʃ 'sɜv ɪn 'wʌn sə'saɪətɪ ər ə'nʌðər əz 'fɔmjuli əv 'gritɪŋ ər ə'proʊtʃ?

aɪ 'θɪŋk ðət, ɪn dɪs'kʌsɪŋ ðə 'fʌŋkʃən əv 'spitʃ ɪn 'mɪə soʊʃə-'bɪlətɪz, wi 'kʌm tə 'wʌn əv ðə 'bɛdrɒk 'aspɛkts əv 'manz 'neɪtʃər ɪn sə'saɪətɪ. ðər ɪz ɪn 'ɔl hjumən 'biɪŋz ðə 'wɛlnoʊn 'tɛndənsɪ tə 'kɒŋgrɪgeɪt, tə bi tə'geðə, tʊ ɪn'dʒɔɪ ɪtʃ ʌðəz 'kʌmpənɪ. 'mɛnɪ 'ɪnstɪŋkts ənd ɪ'neɪt 'trɛndz, sʌtʃ əz 'fɪər ə pʌg'nasətɪ, 'ɔl ðə 'taɪps əv 'soʊʃl 'sɛntɪmənts sʌtʃ əz am'bɪʃn̩, 'vanətɪ, 'paʃn̩ fə 'paʊər ən 'wɛlθ, ə dɪ'pɛndənt əpɒn ənd ə'soʊʃɪeɪtɪd wɪð ðə fʌndə'mɛntl̩ 'tɛndənsɪ wɪtʃ meɪks ðə 'mɪə 'prɛzn̩s əv 'ʌðəz ə nə'sɛsətɪ fə 'man.

naʊ 'spitʃ ɪz ðɪ 'ɪntɪmət 'kɒrəleɪt əv ðɪs 'tɛndənsɪ, 'fɔ, tʊ ə 'natʃrəl 'man, ə'nʌðə manz 'saɪləns ɪz 'nɒt ə rɪə'ʃʊərɪŋ 'faktə, 'bʌt, ɒn ðə 'kɒntrərɪ, sʌmθɪŋ ə'lɑmɪŋ ən 'deɪnʒrəs. ðə 'streɪndʒə hu 'kanɒt 'spik ðə 'laŋgwɪdʒ ɪz tʊ 'ɔl 'savɪdʒ 'traɪbzmən ə 'natʃrəl 'ɛnəmɪ. tə ðə 'prɪmətɪv 'maɪnd, wɛðər əmʌŋ 'savɪdʒɪz ər

47

aʊər 'oʊn ʌn'ɛdjʊkeɪtɪd 'klɑsɪz, tasɪ'tɜnɪtɪ mɪnz 'nɒt oʊnlɪ
ʌn'frɛndlɪnəs bət də'rɛktlɪ ə 'bad 'karɪktə. 'ðɪs noʊ daʊt 'vɛərɪz
'greɪtlɪ wɪð ðə 'naʃənl̩ 'karɪktə bət rɪ'meɪnz 'tru əz ə 'dʒɛnrəl 'rul.
ðə 'breɪkɪŋ əv 'saɪləns, ðə kə'mjunjən əv 'wɜdz ɪz ðə 'fɜst 'akt tʊ
ɪs'tablɪʃ 'lɪŋks əv 'fɛloʊʃɪp, wɪtʃ ɪz 'kɒnsəmeɪtɪd 'oʊnlɪ baɪ ðə
'breɪkɪŋ əv brɛd ən ðə kə'mjunjən əv 'fud. ðə 'mɒdn̩ 'ɪŋglɪʃ
ɪks'prɛʃn̩, "naɪs 'deɪ tədeɪ' ɔ ðə mɛlə'niʒn̩, 'freɪz, "wɛns 'kʌmɪst
ðaʊ?' ɑ 'nɪdɪd tə gɛt 'oʊvə ðə 'streɪnʒ ən ʌn'plɛznt 'tɛnʃən wɪtʃ
mɛn 'fil wɛn 'feɪsɪŋ ɪtʃ ʌðər ɪn 'saɪləns.

ðə kən bɪ 'noʊ 'daʊt ðət wi 'hav hɪər ə 'nju 'taɪp əv lɪŋ'gwɪstɪk
'jus—*fatɪk kə'mjunjən* aɪ m 'tɛmptɪd tə 'kɒl ɪt, 'aktjʊeɪtɪd baɪ ðə
'dɪmən əv 'tɜmɪnə'lɒdʒɪkl̩ ɪn'vɛnʃən—ə 'taɪp əv 'spitʃ ɪn wɪtʃ
'taɪz əv 'junjən ə krɪ'eɪtɪd baɪ ə 'mɪər ɪks'tʃeɪndʒ əv 'wɜdz.

B. MALINOWSKI, 1923

# 5. 'dʒɛstʃəz

'ɛvrɪwʌn ɪz ə'wɛə haɷ 'strɒŋlɪ ðə 'dʒɛstʃəz əv ðə 'handz,
ɪks'prɛʃn̩z əv ðə 'feɪs ənd 'aɪz ən 'bɒdɪ riɪn'fɔs ðə 'spoɷkən
ɪks'tʃeɪndʒ əv 'θɔts ən 'filɪŋz. bət 'nɒt 'ɛvrɪwʌn ɪz 'kɒnʃəs 'haɷ
mʌtʃ ði 'ɪmɪteɪtɪv ənd ɪn'dɪkətɪv 'dʒɛstʃəz ɑ 'sʌbdʒɪkt tə ðə
'vɛərɪəs 'habɪts ən 'juzɪdʒɪz əv 'laŋgwɪdʒ kə'mjunətɪz. 'ðeɪ, 'tu,
həv ə 'kaɪnd əv hɪs'tɒrɪkl̩ 'gramə; ən ðə 'natʃrəl spɒntə'nɪətɪ əv
sʌtʃ 'muvmənts əv ɪks'prɛʃn̩, əv kəmjunɪ'keɪʃn̩ ən rɛprɪzɛn'teɪʃn̩ ɑ
'dɪplɪ ɪn'mɛʃt ɪn ə 'sɪstəm əv 'rulz ðət ɪz kən'tɪnjɷəlɪ dɪ'vɛləpɪŋ ən
'tʃeɪndʒɪŋ. 'oɷld 'frɛnʃ 'dʒɛstʃəz 'dɪfə frəm ðoɷz əv 'mɒdn̩
frɛnʃ; ənd 'ɪf aɷə 'paɷəz əv ɒbzə'veɪʃn̩ həd bɪn 'bɛtə 'treɪnd, wi
'ʃɷd, 'mɪəlɪ frəm ði 'atɪtjudz əv ðə 'feɪsɪz ən 'bɒdɪz əv 'spikəz ən
wɪð'aɷt 'hɪərɪŋ ə 'sɪŋgl̩ 'wɜd, bi 'eɪbl̩ tə 'tɛl ðɛə 'kʌntrɪ ən ðə
'neɪʃn̩ baɪ wɪtʃ ðɛə 'mɪmɪk 'laŋgwɪdʒ həz bɪn 'treɪnd. ən ə'tɛmpt
əz 'rɪsn̩tlɪ bɪn 'meɪd tə rɪ'gad 'ivn̩ ðə 'pəmənənt 'feɪʃl̩ ɪks'prɛʃn̩,
ðə fɪzɪ'ɒnəmɪ ɪn ɪts 'tɪpɪkl̩ 'fɔm, əz ə 'prɒdʌkt əv ðə 'mɪmɪk ənd
ɑtɪkjə'leɪtərɪ 'habɪts əv 'laŋgwɪdʒ. ðʌs ðə 'fraŋkɪʃ feɪs ɪz 'dɪfrənt
tə ðə 'sweɪbjən, 'nɒt bɪkɒz əv ə 'dɪfrəns əv 'reɪs, bət bɪkɒz ɪn ɪt
'dɪfrənt 'laŋgwɪdʒ 'moɷtə 'habɪts həv bɪkʌm 'fɒslaɪzd, əz ɪt 'wɜ.
haɷ 'ʃɑ sʌtʃ ɪg'zampl̩z 'teɪk əs, wi ʃl̩ 'nɒt dɪs'kʌs. wi 'mɪəlɪ 'wɪʃt
tə 'pɒɪnt ət ə 'loɷə 'wɜld, wɛər ə 'saɪlənt 'ʃadoɷ-laŋgwɪdʒ lɪvz
ɪn'taɪəlɪ ɒn ðə 'pleɪ əv 'dʒɛstʃəz, ən 'jɛt ɪn ə'kɒd wɪð 'laŋgwɪdʒ
'juzɪdʒɪz, θru wɪtʃ ðə 'natʃrəl 'muvmənts ɑ 'treɪnd ən 'fɔmd ɪntə
'minz əv ʌndə'standɪŋ wʌn ənʌðə.

K. VOSSLER, 1925, translated by O. Oeser

## 6. ðə ˈdɛf ən kəmjunɪˈkeɪʃn̩

ɪt wəz ɪn ðə ˈsprɪŋ əv ˈeɪtin ˈnaɪntɪ ðət aɪ ˈlɜnt tə ˈspik. ðɪ
ˈɪmpʌls tω ˈʌtər ˈədəbl̩ ˈsaωndz həd ˈɔlwəz bɪn ˈstrɒŋ wɪˈðɪn mɪ.
aɪ ˈjust tə meɪk ˈnɒɪzɪz, kipɪŋ ˈwʌn hand ɒn maɪ ˈθroωt waɪl ðɪ
ˈʌðə hand ˈfɛlt ðə ˈmuvmənts əv maɪ ˈlɪps. aɪ wəz ˈplizd wɪð
ˈɛnɪθɪŋ ðət meɪd ə ˈnɒɪz, ən laɪkt tə ˈfil ðə ˈkat ˈpɜr ən ðə ˈdɒg
ˈbɑk. aɪ ˈɔlsoω laɪkt tə ˈkip maɪ ˈhand ɒn ə ˈsɪŋəz ˈθroωt, ər ɒn ə
ˈpjanoω wɛn ɪt wəz ˈbiɪŋ ˈpleɪd. bɪˈfər aɪ ˈlɒst maɪ ˈsaɪt n̩ ˈhɪərɪŋ,
aɪ wəz ˈfɑst ˈlɜnɪŋ tə ˈtɔk, bət ˈɑftə maɪ ˈɪlnəs ɪt wəz ˈfaωnd ðət
aɪ həd ˈsist tə ˈspik bɪkɒz aɪ ˈkωdn̩t ˈhɪə.

ˈnoω ˈdɛf ˈtʃaɪld hu əz ˈɜnɪstlɪ ˈtraɪd tə ˈspik ðə ˈwɜdz wɪtʃ i əz
ˈnɛvə ˈhɜd—tə ˈkʌm aωt əv ðə ˈprɪzn̩ əv ˈsaɪləns, wɛə ˈnoω ˈtoωn
əv ˈlʌv, ˈnoω ˈsɒŋ əv ˈbɜd, ˈnoω ˈstreɪn əv ˈmjuzɪk ˈɛvə ˈpɪəs ðə
ˈstɪlnəs—kən fəˈgɛt ðə ˈθrɪl əv səˈpraɪz, ðə ˈdʒɒɪ əv dɪsˈkʌvərɪ wɪtʃ
keɪm ˈoωvər ɪm wɛn i ˈʌtəd ɪz ˈfɜst ˈwɜd. ˈoωnlɪ ˈsʌtʃ ə wʌn kən
əˈprɪʃieɪt ðɪ ˈigənəs wɪð wɪtʃ aɪ ˈtəkt tə maɪ ˈtɒɪz, tə ˈstoωnz, ˈtriz,
ˈbɜdz ən ˈdʌm ˈanɪml̩z,ə ðə dɪˈlaɪt aɪ ˈfɛlt wɛn ət maɪ ˈkɔl* ˈmɪldrɪd
ˈran tə mɪ ə maɪ ˈdɒgz əˈbeɪd maɪ kəˈmɑndz. ɪt s ən ʌnˈspikəbl̩
ˈbun tə mɪ tə bi ˈeɪbl̩ tə ˈspik ɪn ˈwɪŋd ˈwɜdz ðət nid ˈnoω ɪntəprɪ-
ˈteɪʃn̩. əz aɪ ˈtɔkt, ˈhapɪ ˈθɔts ˈflʌtəd ˈʌp aωt əv maɪ ˈwɜdz ðət
ˈmaɪt pəhaps əv ˈstrʌgld ɪn ˈveɪn tω ɪsˈkeɪp maɪ ˈfɪŋgəz.

ˈdʒʌst ˈhɪə, pəhaps, aɪ həd ˈbɛtər ɪksˈpleɪn aωə ˈjus əv ðə
ˈmanjωəl ˈalfəbɛt, wɪtʃ ˈsimz tə ˈpʌzl̩ pipl̩ hu ˈdu nɒt ˈnoω əs.
ˈwʌn hu ˈridz ə ˈtɔks tə mɪ ˈspɛlz wɪð ɪz ˈhand, ˈjuzɪŋ ðə ˈsɪŋgl̩-
ˈhand ˈmanjωəl ˈalfəbɛt ˈdʒɛnrəlɪ ɪmˈplɒɪd baɪ ðə ˈdɛf. aɪ ˈpleɪs
ˈmaɪ hand ɒn ðə ˈhand əv ðə ˈspikə soω ˈlaɪtlɪ əz ˈnɒt tə ɪmˈpid
ɪts ˈmuvmənts. ðə pəˈzɪʃn̩ əv ðə ˈhand ɪz əz ˈizɪ tə ˈfil əz ɪt ɪz tə
ˈsi. aɪ ˈdu nɒt ˈfil ˈɪtʃ ˈlɛtə, ˈɛnɪ mə ðən ˈju ˈsi ɪtʃ lɛtə ˈsɛprətlɪ wɛn
ju ˈrid. ˈkɒnstənt ˈpraktɪs meɪks ðə ˈfɪŋgəz vɛrɪ ˈflɛksɪbl̩, ən ˈsʌm

50

## Texts

əv maɪ 'frɛndz 'spɛl 'rapɪdlɪ—əbaʊt əz 'fɑst əz ən 'ɛkspət 'raɪts ɒn ə 'taɪpraɪtə. ðə mɪə 'spɛlɪŋ ɪz, əv kəs, 'noʊ mər ə 'kɒnʃəs 'akt ðən ɪt ɪz ɪn 'raɪtɪŋ.

HELEN KELLER, 1903

# 7. əd'vantɪdʒɪz əv fə'nɛtɪks

ðə 'fɜst ən moʊst 'ɛvɪdn̩t əd'vantɪdʒ əv fə'nɛtɪks ɪz ði ɪndɪ-'pɛndəns ɪt 'gɪvz əs. ɪn ðə 'fɜst pleɪs, ɪt meɪks əs ɪndɪ'pɛndənt əv 'rɛzɪdn̩s ə'brɔd. 'ivn̩ ɪf ðə 'lɜnər ɪn'tɛndz tə 'goʊ tə ðə 'kʌntrɪ wɛə ðə 'laŋgwɪdʒ ɪz 'spoʊkən, ɪt s ə 'greɪt əd'vantɪdʒ tʊ ɪm tə 'stɑt wɪð ə 'θʌrə 'praktɪkl̩ 'nɒlɪdʒ əv ðə 'saʊndz ɪn wɪtʃ i ɪz tə 'praktɪs ɪmsɛlf.

'sɛkəndlɪ, fə'nɛtɪks meɪks əs ɪndɪ'pɛndənt əv 'neɪtɪv 'tɪtʃəz. ɪt s 'sɜtn̩ ðət ə fə'nɛtɪklɪ treɪnd 'ɪŋglɪʃmən hu həz ə 'klɪə 'nɒlɪdʒ əv ðə rə'leɪʃn̩z bɪtwin 'frɛnʃ ənd 'ɪŋglɪʃ 'saʊndz kən tɪtʃ 'frɛnʃ saʊndz tʊ 'ɪŋglɪʃ pipl̩ 'bɛtə ðən ən 'ʌnfənɛtɪk 'frɛnʃmən—stɪl 'mɔ, ən 'ʌnfənɛtɪk 'bɛldʒən, 'swɪs, ə 'poʊl—hu ɪz ʌn'eɪbl̩ tə kə'mjunɪkeɪt ɪz prənʌnsɪ'eɪʃn̩ tʊ ɪz 'pjupl̩z, ən pə'haps spiks ə 'vʌlgər ə daɪə'lɛktl̩ fəm əv 'frɛnʃ ɪm'sɛlf.

ə'gɛn, fə'nɛtɪks ɪ'neɪbl̩z ən ɪn'tɛlɪdʒənt 'adʌlt tə gɛt ə 'saʊnd ɛlɪ'mɛntrɪ 'nɒlɪdʒ əv ðə 'saʊndz əv ə 'fɒrɪn 'laŋgwɪdʒ wɪ'ðaʊt ɛnɪ 'hɛlp frəm aʊt'saɪd—ðat 'ɪz, ɪf i haz ən 'adɪkwət fə'nɛtɪk ə'naləsɪs ən trans'krɪpʃən tə 'wɜk wɪð.

bət ðə 'geɪn əv ə fə'nɛtɪk 'grɑsp əv ə 'laŋgwɪdʒ ɪks'tɛndz 'fa bɪ'jɒnd sʌtʃ 'spɛʃl̩ kənsɪdə'reɪʃn̩z. ə sɪ'kjʊə 'grɑsp əv ðə 'saʊndz əv ə 'laŋgwɪdʒ ɪz ə 'greɪt 'strɛŋθənɪŋ əv ðə 'mastərɪ əv ɪts 'fɔmz ən 'minɪŋz. ə maɪ'njut dɪskrɪmɪ'neɪʃn̩ əv 'sɪmɪlə 'saʊndz ɪn 'kloʊslɪ 'alaɪd 'laŋgwɪdʒɪz ɪz ðə 'ʃʊərɪst 'seɪfgɑd əgɛnst 'ʌðəwaɪz ɪn'ɛvɪtəbl̩ kən'fjuʒn̩z.

'hɛns 'ɔlsoʊ ðə 'lɪtərərɪ ənd is'θɛtɪk jus əv fə'nɛtɪks. fə'nɛtɪks ə'loʊn kən 'brɪð 'laɪf ɪntə ðə 'dɛd 'mas əv 'lɛtəz wɪtʃ 'kɒnstɪtjut ə 'rɪtn̩ 'laŋgwɪdʒ; 'ɪt ə'loʊn kən brɪŋ ðə 'rʌstɪk 'daɪələŋz əv aʊə 'nɒvl̩z bɪfər 'ɛvrɪ ɪn'tɛlɪdʒənt 'ridər əz 'lɪvɪŋ ri'alətɪz, ən 'meɪk əs 'rɪəlaɪz ðə 'lɪvɪŋ 'paʊər ən 'bjutɪ əv ði 'eɪnʃənt 'klasɪkl̩ 'laŋgwɪdʒɪz ɪn 'proʊz ən 'vɜs.

fə'nɛtɪks ɪzn̩t 'mɪəlɪ ən 'ɪndərɛkt 'strɛŋθənər əv grə'matɪkl̩ əsoɷsɪ'eɪʃn̩z, ɪt s ən ɪ'sɛnʃl̩ 'pat əv 'gramər ɪt'sɛlf.

ə 'nɒlɪdʒ əv 'sɛntəns-strɛs ənd ɪntə'neɪʃn̩ ɪz 'nɒt oɷnlɪ ən ɪ'sɛnʃl̩ 'pat əv ɛlə'kjuʃn̩ ən kə'rɛkt prənʌnsɪ'eɪʃn̩, bət ɪt ɪz 'ɔlsoɷ ən 'ɪntəgrəl 'pat əv ðə 'sɪntaks əv 'mɛnɪ 'laŋgwɪdʒɪz.

ɪn 'ʃət, ðər ɪz 'noɷ 'branʃ əv ðə 'stʌdɪ əv 'laŋgwɪdʒ wɪtʃ kən ə'fɔd tə dɪs'pɛns wɪð fə'nɛtɪks.

HENRY SWEET, 1908

## 8. 'spɛlɪŋ rɪfəm

'mɛnɪ əv ði 'advəkəts əv 'spɛlɪŋ rɪfəm ər ɪn ðə 'habɪt əv
ə'sətɪŋ, əː ɪf ɪt wər ən 'aksɪəm əd'mɪtɪŋ əv 'noɷ dɪs'pjut, ðət ðə
'soɷl 'fʌŋkʃən əv 'raɪtɪŋ ɪz tə 'rɛprɪzent 'saɷndz. ɪt ə'pɪəz tə 'mi
ðət ðɪs ɪz 'wʌn əv ðoɷz 'spjɷərɪəs 'truɪzəmz ðət 'ant ɪn'tɛlɪdʒəntlɪ
bə'livd baɪ 'ɛnɪwʌn, bət wɪtʃ kən'tɪnjɷ tə bi rɪ'pitɪd bɪkɒz
'noɷbədɪ teɪks ðə 'trʌbl̩ tə kən'sɪdə wɒt ðeɪ 'rɪəlɪ 'min. aɪ doɷnt
'mɪəlɪ dɪ'naɪ ðə 'truθ əv ðə prɪ'tɛndɪd 'aksɪəm əz ə dɪs'krɪpʃən əv
ðə rɪ'leɪʃn̩z bɪtwin 'spɪtʃ ən 'raɪtɪŋ əz ðəɪ ɪg'zɪst ət ðə 'prɛzn̩t 'deɪ
ɪn 'ɪŋglɪʃ ənd 'ʌðə laŋgwɪdʒɪz. aɪ ə'sət ðət, soɷ 'far əz 'pipl̩z əv
'lɪtərərɪ 'kʌltʃər ə kən'sənd, ðə 'nɛvə 'wɒz ə 'taɪm wɛn 'ðɪs
'fəmjɷlə wɒd əv kə'rɛktlɪ ɪks'prɛst ðə 'fakts; ən ðət ɪt wɒd 'stɪl
rɪmeɪn 'fɒls, 'ivn̩ ɪf ən 'akjərətlɪ fə'nɛtɪk 'spɛlɪŋ həd bɪn ɪn
junɪ'vəsl̩ 'jus fə 'hʌndrədz əv 'jəz.

ɪn 'ədə tɷ ʌndə'stand dɪs'tɪŋktlɪ ðə 'rɪəl 'ɪmpɒt əv ðə 'kʌrn̩t
'steɪtmənt, ɪt wɪl bɪ 'wɛl tə kən'sɪdə ðə 'wʌn 'keɪs ɪn wɪtʃ ɪt s
ɪŋkən'tɛstəblɪ kə'rɛkt. ə 'sɪstəm əv 'mjuzɪkl̩ noɷ'teɪʃn̩ 'kanɒt
'pɛfɪktlɪ fɒl'fɪl ɪts 'pəpəs ənlɛs ɪt s 'soɷ kən'strʌktɪd ðət ɪt wɪl
ɪ'neɪbl̩ ə 'kɒmpɪtn̩t mju'zɪʃn̩ hu əz 'mʌstəd ðə 'sɪstəm tə 'noɷ
ɪg'zaktlɪ, ɒn 'lɷkɪŋ ət ə kɒmpə'zɪʃn̩ 'rɪtn̩ ɪn ðə noɷ'teɪʃn̩, 'wɒt ə
ðə 'saɷndz wɪtʃ ðə kəm'poɷzər ɪn'tɛndɪd hɪz pə'fəmez tə prə-
'djus. 'ɪf ə pis əv 'rɪtn̩ 'mjuzɪk 'dʌzn̩t ə'teɪn ðɪs 'ɛnd wɪð ə
'rizn̩əbl̩ əprɒksɪ'meɪʃn̩ tə kə'rɛktnəs, ɪt s 'jusləs, ən maɪt 'dʒʌst
əz wɛl 'nɒt ɪgzɪst ə 'təl.

naɷ ði ə'səʃn̩ ðət ðə 'soɷl 'fʌŋkʃən əv 'raɪtɪŋ ɪz tə 'rɛprɪzent
'saɷndz ə'maɷnts tə 'seɪɪŋ ðət ðə 'keɪs əv 'rɪtn̩ 'laŋgwɪdʒ ɪz
ɪg'zaktlɪ 'parələl tə ðat əv 'rɪtn̩ 'mjuzɪk. 'ɪf ðɪs bɪ 'soɷ, ɪt məst
'fɒloɷ ðət ən'lɛs ðə 'rɪtn̩ 'fəm əv ən 'ʌnnoɷn 'wəd sə'faɪsɪz tə
kən'veɪ ə 'fɛəlɪ kə'rɛkt 'noɷʃn̩ əv ɪts prənʌnsɪ'eɪʃn̩ tɷ ə 'fɷlɪ
54

ınˈstrʌktıd ˈridə, ðɛn ˈðat ˈwɜd maıt ˈdʒʌst əz wɛl ˈnɒt əv bın
ˈrıtn̩ ə ˈtəl. wi ʃl̩ ˈhav tə ˈseı ðət ə ˈpis əv ˈraıtıŋ ız ˈjusfl̩ ın ðə
prıˈsaıs͏̈ dıˈgri ın wıtʃ ıt ız fəˈnɛtıklı ˈspɛlt, ən ˈnoω ˈfɜðə. pəhaps
ˈnoω wʌn wıl ˈvɛntʃə tə ˈseı ðət ˈðıs ˈsteıtmənt ız ın əˈkɔd wıð ðə
ˈfakts; bət ənˈlɛs ðə ˈkʌrn̩t ˈsjudoω-ˈaksıəm ˈmınz ðıs, aı m ət ə
ˈlɒs tω ıˈmadʒın wɒt ıt ˈkan min. ðə ˈtruθ ˈız ðət bıtwin ˈrıtn̩
ˈmjuzık ən ˈrıtn̩ ˈlaŋgwıdʒ ðər ız ˈwʌn ˈɔlımpətn̩t ˈdıfrəns. ın ˈrıtn̩
ˈmjuzık ðə rɛprızɛnˈteıʃn̩ əv ˈsaωndz ız ði ˈabsəlut ˈʌltımət ˈɛnd.
ın ˈrıtn̩ ˈlaŋgwıdʒ ıt s ˈoωnlı ə ˈminz. wi juz ˈvızəbl̩ ˈsımblz fə ðə
ˈsaωndz əv ˈspıtʃ bıkɒz ˈspoωkən ˈsaωndz ɑ ˈsımblz əv ˈmınıŋ. ði
ˈʌltımət ˈɛnd, ən fə ˈmoωst pɜpəsız, ðoω ˈnɒt fər ˈɔl, ði ˈoωnlı
ımˈpətn̩t ɛnd, əv ˈrıtn̩ ˈlaŋgwıdʒ ız tə kənˈveı ˈmınıŋ. naω ðə dıˈgri
ın wıtʃ ə ˈpis əv ˈraıtıŋ ə ˈprınt ız ˈkeıpəbl̩ əv kənˈveııŋ ıts ˈmınıŋ
ˈdʌznt ə ˈtəl ˈnɛsəsrəlı dıˈpɛnd ɒn ði ˈakjərəsı wıð wıtʃ ıt səˈdʒɛsts
ðə ˈsaωndz ðət wɔd əv bın ˈhɜd ıf ðə kɒmpəˈzıʃn̩ həd bın ˈspoωkən
ınstɛd əv ˈrıtn̩.

Henry Bradley, 1913

# 9. fə'nɛtɪk ə'naləsɪs

ə 'rɪəl ə'naləsɪs əv ðə 'wɜd ɪntɔ ɪts 'prɒpər 'ɛlɪmənts ɪz 'nɒt
mɪəlɪ ɪks'trɪmlɪ 'dɪfɪkḷt, bət ɪz 'aktʃɔəlɪ ɪm'pɒsəbḷ. ə 'wɜd 'ɪzn̩t ə
ju'naɪtɪd 'kɒmpaɔnd əv ə 'dɛfɪnət 'nʌmbər əv ɪndɪ'pɛndənt
'saɔndz, əv wɪtʃ 'ɪtʃ kən bi ɪks'prɛst baɪ ən alfə'bɛtɪkḷ 'saɪn ; bət ɪts
ɪ'sɛnʃəlɪ ə kən'tɪnjɔəs 'sɪərɪz əv 'ɪnfɪnətlɪ 'njumərəs 'saɔndz, ənd
alfə'bɛtɪkḷ 'sɪmbḷz du 'noɔ 'mə ðən 'brɪŋ aɔt 'sətn̩ karɪktə'rɪstɪk
'pɒɪnts əv ðɪs 'sɪərɪz ɪn ən ɪm'pɜfɪkt 'weɪ. ðə rɪ'meɪndə, wɪtʃ
rɪ'meɪnz ʌndɪ'noɔtɪd, noɔ daɔt 'nɛsɪsrəlɪ rɪ'vɪlz ɪtsɛlf frəm ðə
dɛfn̩'ɪʃn̩ əv ðɪz 'pɒɪnts, bət rɪ'vɪlz ɪtsɛlf 'oɔnlɪ ʌp tɔ ə 'sɜtn 'pɒɪnt.
ðə kɒntɪn'jɔətɪ əv 'saɔnd ɪz sin wɪð ðə 'greɪtɪst 'klɪənəs ɪn ðə
'keɪs əv ðə 'soɔ-kəld 'dɪfθɒŋz, wɪtʃ ɪg'zɪbɪt 'sʌtʃ ə 'sɪərɪz əv 'vɛrɪ
'njumərəs 'ɛlɪmənts. bət ɪt 'fɒloɔz frəm ðɪs kɒntɪn'jɔətɪ əv ðə
'wɜd ðət ən aɪ'dɪə əv ði ɪndɪ'vɪdʒɔəl 'pɑts 'kanɒt bi ə 'sɛlf-'jɪldɪd
rɪ'zʌlt, bət 'mʌst bɪ ðə 'frut əv saɪən'tɪfɪk rɪ'flɛkʃən, haɔ'ɛvə
'prɪmətɪv ðɪs meɪ 'bi, ənd ɪt ɪz ðə 'praktɪkḷ 'nid əv 'raɪtɪŋ tɔ
ɪks'prɛs 'saɔndz wɪtʃ əz kən'djust tə ðɪs.

H. PAUL, 1886, translated by H. A. Strong

56

# 10. 'mitər ın 'proɯz

'mitə, ın ðə 'praımərı dı'gri əv ə 'sımpļ 'sıəriz əv aı'sɒkrənəs
'ıntəvḷz, 'mɑkt baı 'aksənts, ız əz 'natʃrəl tə 'spoɯken 'laŋgwıdʒ
əz ən 'ivņ 'peıs ız tə 'wəkıŋ. 'proɯz dı'lıvərı, wı'ðaɯt ðıs ə'maɯnt
əv 'mitə, ız laık ə 'drʌŋkədz 'wək, ði ıregjɯ'larıtı əv wıtʃ ız 'soɯ
fɑ frəm biıŋ 'natʃrəl tɯ ə 'pɜsņ ın ız 'sɛnsız, ðət ıt 'ızņt ivņ tə bi
'ımıteıtıd wıðaɯt 'ɛfət. naɯ, əz 'dansıŋ ız noɯ 'mə ðən ən 'ıŋkris
əv ði 'ɛlımənt əv 'mɛʒə wıtʃ əl'rɛdı ıg'zısts ın 'wəkıŋ, 'soɯ 'vɜs ız
bət ən ə'dıʃņļ dı'gri əv ðat 'mitə wıtʃ ız ın'hıərənt ın 'proɯz
'spikıŋ.

ðə 'mɛtrıkļ ən 'mjuzıkļ 'lɔ ın 'proɯz həz bın dısrı'gɑdıd ņ
fə'gɒtņ, bıkɒz ıts 'neıtʃər ız soɯ 'sımpļ ðət ıts əb'zɜvņs meı bı
'seıflı 'trʌstıd tɯ 'ınstıŋkt, ən rı'kwaıəz 'noɯ 'eıd frəm taıpə-
'grafıkļ dı'vıʒņz. 'prɒbəblı 'mɛnı əv maı 'ridəz wıl 'fil əz 'mʌtʃ
sə'praızd ət 'lɜnıŋ ðət deı v bın 'spikıŋ ın 'mitər 'əl ðɛə 'laıvz, əz
ðə *'boɯʒwɑ *'ʒɒntıjɒm fɛlt ɒn biıŋ 'toɯld ðət i 'wɒz, wı'ðaɯt
ın'strʌkʃən, ın ðə 'habıt əv 'təkıŋ 'proɯz. aı 'sɜtņlı 'kanɒt ıks'pɛkt
ðəm tə bə'liv soɯ 'statlıŋ ə prɒpə'zıʃņ əpɒn maı 'mıər ə'sɜʃņ: aı
məst ə'lɛdʒ ə 'fju 'prufs, prı'maızıŋ, haɯɛvə, ðət ðə 'mɛlədı, ər
'ɛlımənt əv 'toɯn ın 'laŋgwıdʒ, ız 'soɯ ın'sɛprəblı kə'nɛktıd wıð
ıts 'mitər ə 'taım, ðət ðə 'tu 'θıŋz wıl 'skɛəslı kən'sɛnt tə bı
kən'sıdəd 'sɛprətlı. baı ðə 'mitər ən 'mɛlədı əv 'proɯz, aı əv kɒs
'min ðə 'mitər ən 'mɛlədı wıtʃ ıg'zısts ın ðə 'kɒmən ənd ın'tɛlı-
dʒəbļ dı'lıvərı ɒv ıt. 'vɜs ıt'sɛlf ız 'oɯnlı 'vɜs ɒn ðə kən'dıʃņ əv
'raıt 'rıdıŋ: wi 'meı, ıf wi 'tʃuz, 'rid ðə moɯst 'pɜfıkt 'vɜs soɯ ðət
'əl ði ı'fɛkt əv 'vɜs ʃļ bı 'lɒst. ðə 'seım 'θıŋ meı bı 'dʌn wıð 'proɯz.
wi meı 'klıəlı ɑ'tıkjɯleıt 'əl ðə 'sıləbḷz, ən prı'zɜv ðɛə 'dju kə'nɛkʃən ın ðə 'freızız ðeı 'kɒnstıtjut; ən 'jɛt, baı nı'glɛktıŋ tə 'gıv ðəm
ðɛə 'rɛlətıv 'toɯnz, ən tə 'grup ðəm ə'kɒdıŋ tə 'taım, kən'vɜt ðəm

57

frəm 'proʊz ıntə sʌmθıŋ 'neımləs, əb'sɜd, ənd ʌnın'tɛlıdʒəbl̩.
soʊ 'fɑr ız ıt frəm biıŋ 'tru ðət ðə 'taım ən 'toʊn əv 'proʊz 'rıdıŋ
ən 'spikıŋ ə wı'ðaʊt 'lɔ, ðət ðɛə 'lɔz ə 'mə 'strıkt ðən 'ðoʊz əv
'gramər ıt'sɛlf. ðər ə 'nɛvə 'tu 'ikwəlı 'gɒd 'weız əv 'rıdıŋ ə
sɛntəns, ðoʊ ðə meı bı 'hɑf ə 'dʌzn̩ əv 'raıtıŋ ıt. ıf 'wʌn ən ðə
'seım 'sɛntəns ız 'rıdəbl̩ ın 'mə ðən 'wʌn 'weı, ıt s bıkɒz ıt haz 'mə
ðən 'wʌn 'pɒsəbl̩ 'minıŋ. "ʃal ju wɔk 'aʊt tədeı?' ız ə 'kwɛstʃən
wıtʃ meı bı 'ɑskt wıð əz 'mɛnı vɛərı'eıʃn̩z əv 'strɛs ən 'toʊn əz ðər
ɑ 'wɜdz ın ıt; bət 'ɛvrı vɛərı'eıʃn̩ ınvɒlvz ə vɛərı'eıʃn̩ əv 'minıŋ.

C. PATMORE, 1856

## 11. 'poɯɪtrɪ 'spoɯkən ən 'rɪtn̩

'wɛn, ðɛəfə, wi kən'sɪdə ðə fə'nɛtɪk 'aspɛkt əv 'poɯɪtrɪ, ɪts
'ɒbvɪəs ðət wi ə'sjum ðə 'spoɯkən ɪg'zɪstəns əv 'laŋgwɪdʒ; 'soɯ
ɒbvɪəs ðət ɪt maɪt 'hɑdlɪ sim 'wɜθ 'mɛnʃn̩ɪŋ. bət wɪ ə 'sʌmtaɪmz
'apt tə fə'gɛt, 'ivn̩ ɪn 'ðɪs kə'nɛkʃən, ðət 'laŋgwɪdʒ 'haz, ənd 'haz
had fə 'mɛnɪ 'sɛntʃərɪz, ə 'dʌbl̩ 'laɪf, ɪn 'poɯɪtrɪ əz ɛls'wɛə.
'laŋgwɪdʒ 'lɪvz əz ðə 'spoɯkən wɜd, ənd ɪt lɪvz əz 'ɔlsoɯ əz ðə 'rɪtn̩
(ə 'prɪntɪd) wɜd. ðə 'spoɯkən wɜd 'kanɒt bi 'ɛnɪθɪŋ 'ɛls ðən
'saɯnd ək'sɛptɪd əz ðə 'sɪmbl̩ əv ən aɪ'dɪə; ən ðə 'rɪtn̩ wɜd wəz
ə'rɪdʒɪnlɪ ðə sɪmbl̩ əv ðɪs 'spoɯkən 'saɯnd: 'ðats tə seɪ, ðə
'sɪmbl̩ əv ðə 'sɪmbl̩ əv ən aɪ'dɪə. bət ðə 'rɪtn̩ wɜd 'kan bi, ən həz
'lɒŋ sins ɪn 'pat bɪ'kʌm, sʌmθɪŋ 'ɛls ðən ðə 'sɪmbl̩ 'ɒv ə sɪmbl̩;
ɪt kən bi ə 'sɪmbl̩ ɪn ɪts 'oɯn 'raɪt. fə ðə 'hlumən 'maɪnd wɪl
'ɔlwəz 'ʃɔt-'sɜkɪt ə 'proɯsɛs wɛn ɪt 'kan. əz 'sun əz ðə 'habɪt əv
'rɪdɪŋ tɔ wʌn'sɛlf wəz ɪs'tablɪʃt, ðə 'sɛkənd-'hand 'sɪmbəlɪzəm
əv ðə 'rɪtn̩ 'wɜd wəz 'ʃɔt-'sɜkɪtɪd; ən ðə 'rɪtn̩ 'wɜd bɪkeɪm ɪt'sɛlf
ðə 'sɪmbl̩ əv ði aɪ'dɪə, wɪ'ðaɯt havɪŋ tə 'pas θru ðə 'sɪmbəlɪzəm əv
'saɯnd. 'prɪntɪŋ həz 'fɪkst ðɪs 'ʃɔt-'sɜkɪt ɪn aɯə 'sɪvəlaɪzd mɛn-
'talətɪ soɯ 'dɪplɪ ðət 'mɛnɪ ɒv əs ə 'skɛəslɪ ə'wɛər əv ɪt.

'laŋgwɪdʒ, əz kə'mjunɪkəbl̩ 'sɪmbəlɪzəm əv aɪ'dɪəz, həz 'tu
'moɯdz əv ɪg'zɪstəns: ɪt ɪg'zɪsts əz 'ɔdəbl̩ saɪnz ən ɪt ɪg'zɪsts əz
'vɪzəbl̩ saɪnz. 'dʒɛnrəlɪ, ði 'oɯnlɪ 'praktɪkl̩ rɪ'leɪʃn̩ bɪtwin ðə 'tu
kaɪndz əv 'saɪnz ɪz ðət ðeɪ'boɯθ rɪ'fɜ tə ðə 'seɪm 'θɪŋ: ði 'ɪŋglɪʃ wɪ
'rid həz 'ɔlmoɯst gɪvn̩ 'ʌp prɪ'tɛndɪŋ tə hav 'ɛnɪθɪŋ tə 'du wɪð ði
'ɪŋglɪʃ wɪ 'hɪə. əz ə 'rul, 'wɛn wɪ ə 'rɪdɪŋ tɔ aɯə'sɛlvz, ðə 'prɪntɪd
'wɜd rɪ'fɜz ɪ'mɪdʒətlɪ tɔ ɪts aɪ'dɪə; ðə 'saɯnd əv ðə wɜd 'vɛrɪ
'laɪklɪ kʌmz 'ɪn, bət ɪts 'nɒt rɪ'kwaɪəd, ən 'meɪ bɪ 'dju tɔ
əsoɯsɪ'eɪʃn̩ wɪð ði aɪ'dɪə əz 'mʌtʃ əz tə 'teɪkɪŋ ðə 'lɛtəz əz fə'nɛtɪk
'saɪnz. ðə 'saɯnd əv ðə wɜd ət 'ɛnɪ reɪt 'oɯnlɪ kʌmz 'ɪn əz ə 'feɪnt

ʌn'nɛsəsrɪ ə'kʌmpnɪmənt, tə wɪtʃ wi 'oɷnlɪ ə'tɛnd əz ə sət əv
'maɪld kərɒbə'reɪʃn̩. 'bʌt, ðoɷ ɪt meɪ bɪ 'prɒpər ɪ'nʌf tə rid aɷə
'njuspeɪpəz ɪn ðat 'staɪl, ɪt wɪl 'nɒt du fə 'poɷɪtrɪ. 'poɷɪtrɪ kənsɪsts
'absəlutlɪ əv ðə 'wɛd 'spoɷkən ən 'hɜd: ðə 'prɪntɪd wɜd məst
'ɔlwəz bɪ 'fraŋklɪ ðə 'sɪmbl̩ əv ɑ'tɪkjələt 'saɷnd. wɪ məst 'hɪə wɒt
ðə 'poɷɪt haz tə 'seɪ; ɪf wɪ ə 'rɪdɪŋ tɷ aɷə'sɛlvz, wɪ məst 'hɪər ɪt
'mɛntəlɪ. 'ʌðəwaɪz wɪ ʃl̩ 'mɪs 'haf hɪz tɛk'nik; ən 'ðat mɪnz, wɪ
ʃl̩ mɪs 'haf əv wɒt hi z 'traɪɪŋ tɷ ɪks'prɛs.

bət ðər ɪz 'stɪl 'sʌmθɪŋ tə bɪ 'sɛd ɒn ðɪs 'matə; ðə 'vɪzəbl̩ wɜd
'ɪzn̩t tə bɪ dɪs'mɪst ɪn 'poɷɪtrɪ ɔltə'gɛðə, ɪn 'feɪvər əv ði 'ɒdəbl̩ wɜd.
ðəz 'noɷ 'daɷt, ɪn fakt, ðət ði ɪg'zɪstəns əv 'laŋwɪdʒ əz 'prɪntɪd
'wɜdz həz had ə prə'faɷnd 'ɪnflɷəns ɒn ði 'at əv 'poɷɪtrɪ, ðoɷ ɪt
wɒd 'teɪk tu 'lɒŋ tɷ ɪn'vɛstɪgeɪt ðɪs 'hɪər ɪg'zaktlɪ. wi 'rid
'poɷɪtrɪ tɷ aɷə'sɛlvz mər 'ɒfn̩ ðən 'hɪər ɪt 'rɛd ə'laɷd; ən 'poɷɪts,
'kɒnʃəslɪ ə 'nɒt, həv 'teɪkən əd'vantɪdʒ əv ðɪs. 'poɷɪtrɪ wɪl
'ɔlwəz teɪk əd'vantɪdʒ əv 'ɛnɪθɪŋ ðət wɪl ɪŋ'kris ə rɪ'faɪn ɪts
ɪks'prɛsɪv 'paɷə. aɪ 'sɛd, ðət ðə 'prɪntɪd 'wɜd ɪn 'poɷɪtrɪ məst
'ɔlwəz bɪ 'teɪkən əz ə 'sɪmbl̩ əv ən ɑ'tɪkjələt 'saɷnd. aɪ 'dɪd nɒt
seɪ, ɪt kəd 'oɷnlɪ bɪ teɪkən soɷ. wɛn wɪ 'rid 'poɷɪtrɪ tɷ aɷə'sɛlvz,
ɪt s 'nɒt, aɪ θɪŋk, ðə 'juʒɷəl θɪŋ tə rɪ'fɜ ðə 'wɜd tə ðə 'saɷnd ən
'ðɛns, 'θru ðə saɷnd, tə ði aɪ'dɪə; aɪ 'θɪŋk raðə wɪ rɪ'fɜ ðə 'prɪntɪd
wɜd ɪ'mɪdʒətlɪ tə ði aɪ'dɪə ən sɪml̩'teɪnjəslɪ tə ðə 'saɷnd əz 'wɛl. ən
'ðɪs ɪz ɪm'pɒtn̩t; fər 'aɪ-laŋwɪdʒ ɪz ə mʌtʃ 'sʌtʃər ən 'nɪmblər
ə'feə ðən 'ɪə-laŋwɪdʒ. wi kən 'gɛt, ɪn 'prɪntɪd laŋwɪdʒ, ɪn ði
ə'pɪl θru ði 'aɪ, ə mər 'ɪnstənt ən mə 'sɜtn̩ aprɪ'hɛnʃən əv 'faɪn
əsoɷsɪ'eɪʃn̩z əv aɪ'dɪəz, əv 'dɛlɪkət 'ʃeɪdz əv sɪg'nɪfɪkəns, ðən ju
kən 'ɛvə gɛt θru ði 'ɪə.

L. ABERCROMBIE, 1924

# 12. 'gɒd 'ɪŋglɪʃ

'gɒd 'ɪŋglɪʃ ɪz 'pleɪn, 'izɪ, ən 'smuð ɪn ðə 'maɷθ əv ən 'ʌnəfɛktɪd 'ɪŋglɪʃ 'dʒɛntlmən. ə 'stʌdɪd n̩ fak'tɪʃəs prənʌnsɪ'eɪʃn̩, wɪtʃ rɪ'kwaɪəz pə'pɛtʃɷəl ə'tɛnʃən, ənd ɪm'pɷɷzɪz pə'pɛtʃɷəl kən-'streɪnt, ɪz ɪk'sidɪŋlɪ dɪs'gʌstɪŋ. ə 'sməl ɪntə'mɪkstʃər əv prə'vɪnʃəl pɪkjulɪ'arɪtɪz 'meɪ, pəhaps, hav ən ə'grɪəbl̩ ɪ'fɛkt, əz ðə 'nɷɷts əv 'dɪfrənt 'bɜdz kən'kɜr ɪn ðə 'hɑmənɪ əv ðə 'grɷɷv, ən 'pliz 'mə ðən ɪf ðeɪ wər 'əl ɪg'zaktlɪ ə'laɪk. aɪ kɷd 'neɪm səm 'dʒɛntlmən əv 'aɪələnd, tə hum ə 'slaɪt prə'pəʃn̩ əv ði 'aksənt ən rɛsɪtə'tɪv əv ðat 'kʌntrɪ ɪz ən əd'vɑntɪdʒ. ðə 'seɪm ɒbzə'veɪʃn̩z wɪl ə'plaɪ tə ðə 'dʒɛntlmən əv 'skɒtlənd. aɪ 'du nɒt 'min ðət wi ʃɷd 'spik əz 'brɒd əz ə 'sɜtn̩ 'prɒspərəs 'mɛmbər əv 'pɑləmənt frəm ðat 'kʌntrɪ; ðɷɷ ɪt əz bɪn 'wɛl əb'zɜvd, ðət 'ɪt əz bɪn əv 'nɷɷ 'sməl 'jus tɷ ɪm, əz ɪt 'raɷzɪz ði ə'tɛnʃən əv ðə 'haɷs baɪ ɪts ʌn'kɒmənnəs; ənd ɪz 'ikwəl tə 'trɷɷps ən 'fɪgəz ɪn ə gɷd 'ɪŋglɪʃ spikə'. aɪ wɷd 'gɪ vəz ən 'ɪnstəns əv wɒt aɪ 'min tə rɛkə'mɛnd tə maɪ 'kʌntrɪmən, ðə prənʌnsɪ'eɪʃn̩ əv ðə 'leɪt sə *'gɪlbət *'ɛlɪət; ən 'meɪ aɪ prɪ'zjum tɷ 'ad 'ðat əv ðə 'prɛznt̩ 'ɜl əv *'mɑtʃmənt, hu 'tɷɷld mɪ wɪð 'greɪt gɷd 'hjumə, ðət ðə 'mɑstər əv ə 'ʃɒp ɪn 'lʌndən, wɛə hi wəz 'nɒt 'nɷɷn, 'sɛd tɷ ɪm, 'aɪ sə'pɷɷz, sə, jɷ ər ən ə'mɛrɪkən'. 'waɪ 'sɷɷ, sə?' sɛd ɪz 'lədʃɪp. 'bɪ'kɒz, sə,' rɪplaɪd ðə 'ʃɒpkipə, 'ju 'spik naɪðər 'ɪŋglɪʃ nə 'skɒtʃ, bət sʌmθɪŋ 'dɪfrənt frəm 'bɷɷθ, wɪtʃ aɪ kən'klud ɪz ðə 'laŋgwɪdʒ əv ə'mɛrɪkə.'

J. BOSWELL, 1791

61

## 13. *ˈhɛnrɪ *ˈswit

ðɪ ˈɪŋglɪʃ həv ˈnoʊ rɪsˈpɛkt fə ðɛə ˈlaŋgwɪdʒ, ən ˈwɪl nɒt ˈtitʃ
ðɛə ˈtʃʊldrən tə ˈspik ɪt. ðeɪ ˈkanɒt ˈspɛl ɪt bɪkɒz ðeɪ həv ˈnʌθɪŋ
tə ˈspɛl ɪt wɪð bət ən ˈoʊld ˈfɒrɪn ˈalfəbɛt əv wɪtʃ ˈoʊnlɪ ðə ˈkɒn-
sənənts—ən ˈnɒt əl əv ˈðɛm—həv ˈɛnɪ əˈgrid ˈspitʃ valjʊ. ˈkɒn-
sɪkwəntlɪ ˈnoʊ man kən ˈtitʃ ɪmsɛlf wɒt ɪt ʃʊd ˈsaʊnd laɪk frəm
ˈridɪŋ ɪt; ənd ɪt s ɪmˈpɒsəbļ fər ən ˈɪŋglɪʃmən tʊ ˈoʊpən ɪz ˈmaʊθ
wɪˈðaʊt meɪkɪŋ sʌm ˈʌðər ɪŋglɪʃmən dɪsˈpaɪz ɪm. ˈmoʊst
ˈjʊərəpɪən ˈlaŋgwɪdʒɪz ə ˈnaʊ əkˈsɛsəbļ ɪn ˈblak ən ˈwaɪt tə
ˈfɒrɪnəz: ˈɪŋglɪʃ ən ˈfrɛnʃ ɑ ˈnɒt ˈðʌs əkˈsɛsəbļ ˈivn̩ tʊ ˈɪŋglɪʃmən
ən ˈfrɛnʃmən. ðə rɪˈfɔmə wi nid ˈmoʊst təˈdeɪ ɪz ən ɛnəˈdʒɛtɪk
ɪnˈθjuzɪast: ˈðat ɪz waɪ aɪ v ˈmeɪd sʌtʃ ə wʌn ðə ˈhɪəroʊ əv ə
ˈpɒpjʊlə ˈpleɪ.

ðər əv bɪn ˈhɪəroʊz əv ðat ˈkaɪnd ˈkraɪɪŋ ɪn ðə ˈwɪldənəs fə
ˈmɛnɪ ˈjɜz ˈpɑst. ˈwɛn aɪ bɪkeɪm ˈɪntrəstɪd ɪn ðə ˈsʌbdʒɪkt tədz ðɪ
ˈɛnd əv ðɪ ˈeɪtɪn-ˈsɛvn̩tɪz, ðɪ ɪˈlʌstrɪəs *alɪgˈzandə *ˈmɛlvɪl *ˈbɛl,
ðɪ ɪnˈvɛntər əv ˈvɪzəbļ ˈspitʃ, həd ˈɛmɪgreɪtɪd tə ˈkanədə, wɛər ɪz
ˈsʌn ɪnˈvɛntɪd ðə ˈtɛlɪfoʊn; bət *alɪgˈzandə *ˈdʒeɪ *ˈɛlɪs wəz ˈstɪl
ə ˈlʌndən ˈpeɪtriak, wɪð ən ɪmˈprɛsɪv ˈhɛd ˈɔlwəz ˈkʌvəd baɪ ə
ˈvɛlvɪt ˈskʌl kap, fə ˈwɪtʃ i wʊd əˈpɒlədʒaɪz tə ˈpʌblɪk ˈmitɪŋz ɪn ə
ˈvɛrɪ ˈkətlɪ ˈmanə. ˈhi ən *ˈtitoʊ *paljaˈdini, əˈnʌðə fəˈnɛtɪk
ˈvɛtərən, wə ˈmɛn hum ɪt wəz ɪmˈpɒsəbļ tə dɪsˈlaɪk. *ˈhɛnrɪ *ˈswit,
ˈðɛn ə ˈjʌŋ ˈman, ˈlakt ðɛə ˈswitnəs əv ˈkarɪktə: hi wəz əbaʊt əz
kənˈsɪljətrɪ tə kənˈvɛnʃənļ ˈmətļz əz *ˈɪbsən ə *ˈsamjʊəl *ˈbʌtlə.
hɪz ˈgreɪt əˈbɪlətɪ əz ə foʊnəˈtɪʃn̩ (hi ˈwɒz, aɪ θɪŋk, ðə ˈbɛst əv ðəm
ˈɔl ət ɪz ˈdʒɒb) wʊd əv ɪnˈtaɪtļd ɪm tə ˈhaɪ əˈfɪʃļ rɛkəgˈnɪʃn̩, ən
pəˈhaps ɪˈneɪbļd ɪm tə ˈpɒpjʊləraɪz ɪz ˈsʌbdʒɪkt, ˈbʌt fər ɪz
səˈtanɪk kənˈtɛmpt fər ˈɔl akəˈdɛmɪk ˈdɪgnətrɪz ən ˈpɜsn̩z ɪn
ˈdʒɛnrəl hu θət ˈmɔr əv ˈgrik ðən əv fəˈnɛtɪks.

BERNARD SHAW, 1920

## 14. lıŋ'gwıstık 'tɒlərəns

wi məst 'lɜn tə bıkʌm 'mə 'tɒlərənt əv ðə 'wɜd əz 'spoʊkən baı ə'mɛrıkənz, kə'neıdiənz, ɒs'treıljənz, ən saʊθ 'afrıkənz; ənd 'ıŋglıʃ-spikıŋ 'lısnəz ɒn ði 'ʌðə saıd əv ðə 'wɜldz 'oʊʃnz məst rı'mɛmbə ðət 'wɛn ıt kʌmz tə 'θroʊıŋ 'stoʊnz ət ðə 'soʊ-kəld 'brıtıʃ ıŋglıʃ, 'ðeı, 'tu, lıv ın 'glɑs 'haʊzız. ði 'ıŋglıʃ 'laŋgwıdʒ ız ə 'vɛrı mʌtʃ mə 'waıdsprɛd 'laŋgwıdʒ ðən ðə 'wɜld həz 'jɛt 'sin ın ıts 'hıstrı, ən ðə 'fɜst θıŋ ði 'ıŋglıʃ-spikıŋ 'pipļz hav tə 'lɜn ız ðət ðər ə 'mɛnı 'gʊd 'weız əv 'spikıŋ ıt. 'ɛvrıbɒdı bə'livz ız 'oʊn tə bı ðə 'bɛst, ən 'atıtjud ðət, ın 'ʌðə 'sfıəz əv 'laıf, sıvəlaı'zeıʃn əz 'tət əs tə dıs'paız. 'mɛnı 'naʃņļ 'mısʌndə'standıŋz ə 'dju tə 'sımpļ 'laŋgwıdʒ 'dıfrənsız, əz 'ıvņ ə 'ʃət kəm'parətıv ınvɛsti'geıʃņ ıntʊ 'ıŋglıʃ ənd ə'mɛrıkən ıntə'neıʃņ wıl kən'vıns 'ɛnıbɒdı. 'mɛni ə'mɛrıkənz ər ə'fɛndıd baı ðə 'nəmļ ıntə'neıʃņz əv 'brıtıʃ 'ıŋglıʃ, dʒʌst əz 'brıtıʃəz ər 'ɒfņ 'hɜt baı ə'mɛrıkən ıntəneıʃņz. mʌtʃ əv aʊə 'heıstı dʒɛnrəlaı'zeıʃņ kənsənıŋ ðə 'frɛnʃ 'tɛmprəmənt ız 'dju tə ðə 'fakt ðət 'frɛnʃ 'spikəz 'juz, ın 'nəmļ 'sɜkəmstənsız, 'taıps əv ıntə'neıʃņ ðət ər ın 'ıŋglıʃ ə'soʊʃıeıtıd wıð sıtʃʊ'eıʃņz ðət ə 'nɒt nəmļ. wı ər 'ɔl soʊ sə'sɛptəbļ tə ðə maı'njutıst 'dıteılz əv 'spıtʃ bıheıvjə, ðət wɛn'ɛvə wi əb'zɜv ðə 'spıtʃ bıheıvjər əv 'ʌðəz, wi ı'madʒın ðəm tə bı 'sʌfərıŋ frəm ðə 'seım ı'moʊʃņz əz 'wi ʃəd hav tə 'sʌfə frɒm bıfə 'wi bıheıvd əz 'ðeı du. ənd əz ə 'rul, ıt s ði ıntə'neıʃņ ðət 'hɜts; 'ıŋglıʃ spoʊkən ɒn 'swidıʃ ıntəneıʃņ meı saʊnd 'pɛtjʊlənt, ɒn 'rʌʃņ ıntəneıʃņ lə'gubrıəs, ɒn 'dʒɜmən ıntəneıʃņ ə'fɛnsıv, ɒn 'frɛnʃ ıntəneıʃņ ʌgjʊ'mɛntətıv, ɒn 'mɛnı ə'mɛrıkən ıntəneıʃņz 'kaʒjʊəļ ə 'kɒk'ʃʊə, ɒn 'deınıʃ ıntəneıʃņ 'flat ņ 'sɒmbə. 'wɒt 'fɒrın laŋgwıdʒız 'saʊnd laık wɛn 'spoʊkən ɒn 'brıtıʃ ər ə'mɛrıkən 'spıtʃ 'rıðəmz ənd ıntə'neıʃņz ız 'bɛst 'lɛft tʊ ə 'laıvlı ımadʒı'neıʃņ; 'mɛnı əv ðə 'pɒpjʊlər ə'pınjənz 'hɛld

63

baɪ ˈfɒrɪn ˈneɪʃn̩z əv ði ˈɪŋglɪʃmən ə ˈdju tʊ ˈɪŋglɪʃ ɪntəˈneɪʃn̩z, wɪtʃ meɪ səˈdʒɛst əˈfɛnsɪv ˈhɒtɪnəs ər ˈɪmpjʊdn̩s tə ˈpɪpl̩ hu həˈbɪtʃʊəlɪ juz ˈʌðər ɪntəneɪʃn̩z. ən ðə ˈlaʊd ˈvɒɪs ɪn wɪtʃ ˈmɛnɪ ˈɪŋglɪʃ ənd əˈmɛrɪkən ˈmɛn ən ˈwɪmɪn ər ɪn ðə ˈhabɪt əv kən-ˈdʌktɪŋ ˈpraɪvət kɒnvəˈseɪʃn̩ ɪn ˈpʌblɪk ˈpleɪsɪz meɪ hav ˈmɔ ˈsɪərɪəs ˈkɒnsɪkwənsɪz ðən ðat əv ˈrʌflɪŋ kənˈdʌktəz ɪn ˈkɒvn̩t ˈgɑdn̩. ðə ˈvɒljʊm əv əˈfɛns ðət ɪt ˈkɔzɪz ɒn ðə ˈmeɪnland əv ˈjʊərəp wʊd bɪ ˈhɑd tə ˈmɛʒə.

ˈðɪs, pəhaps, ɪz ðə ˈgreɪtɪst ˈdeɪnʒər əv ðə ˈspoʊkən ˈwɜd; ðə ˈtɛknɪkl̩ ˈditeɪlz əv ɪts ˈʌtərəns, əv ˈlɪtl̩ sɪgˈnɪfɪkəns tə ðə ˈspikə, meɪ əˈraʊz ɪn ðə ˈmaɪndz əv lɪsn̩əz ɪˈmoʊʃn̩z ˈfɑ ˈdɪfrənt frəm ˈðoʊz ðət ˈprɒmpt ɪt ɪn ðə ˈmaɪnd əv ðə ˈspikə. ɪnˈdid ɪt meɪ ˈbi ðət ðə ˈprɪntɪd wɜd ɪz ˈseɪfə fər ɪntəˈnaʃn̩l̩ ˈkʌrn̩sɪ əntɪl ðə ˈwɜld həz ˈlɜnt, ɪf ˈnɒt tə ˈstandədaɪz ðə rɪˈleɪʃn̩ bɪtwin ɪˈmoʊʃn̩ ənd ɪntəˈneɪʃn̩, ət ˈɛnɪ reɪt tə bɪˈheɪv ɪn ðɪ ɪntəˈnaʃn̩l̩ lɪŋˈgwɪstɪk ˈpleɪgraʊnd ˈlɛs laɪk ðə ˈbeɪbɪz ɪn ən ˈɪnfənts ˈskul ˈpleɪgraʊnd.

A. LLOYD JAMES, 1935

ðə wəz 'wʌns ə 'jʌŋ 'rat neɪmd 'aθə, hu wɒd 'nɛvə teɪk ðə
'trʌbl̩ tə 'meɪk ʌp ɪz 'maɪnd. wɛn'ɛvər ɪz 'frɛndz 'askt ɪm ɪf hi
wɒd 'laɪk tə goɷ 'aɷt wɪð ðəm, hi wɒd 'oɷnlɪ 'ansə, 'aɪ 'doɷnt
'noɷ.' hi 'wɒdn̩t seɪ "jɛs', ənd i wɒdn̩t seɪ "noɷ' 'aɪðə. hi kɒd
'nɛvə 'lɜn tə 'meɪk ə 'tʃɒɪs.

hɪz 'ant \*'hɛlɪn 'sɛd tə hɪm, "noɷ wʌn wɪl 'ɛvə 'kɛə fə jɷ ɪf ju
'karɪ ɒn laɪk 'ðɪs. ju həv 'noɷ mə 'maɪnd ðən ə 'bleɪd əv 'gras.'
'aθə lɒkt 'waɪz, bət 'sɛd 'nʌθɪŋ.

'wʌn 'reɪnɪ 'deɪ ðə 'rats həd ə 'greɪt 'nɒɪz ɪn ðə 'lɒft wɛə ðeɪ
'lɪvd. ðə 'paɪn 'raftəz wər 'əl 'rɒtn̩, ənd ət 'last 'wʌn əv ðə
'dʒɒɪsts həd 'gɪvn̩ 'weɪ ən 'fɒlən tə ðə 'graɷnd. ðə 'wɒlz 'ʃɒk, ənd
'əl ðə rats 'hɛə 'stɒd ɒn 'ɛnd wɪð 'fɪər ən 'hɒrə. "ðɪs woɷnt 'du,'
sɛd ði 'oɷld 'rat hu wəz 'tʃif. 'aɪl 'sɛnd aɷt 'skaɷts tə 'sɜtʃ fər ə
'nju 'hoɷm.'

'θri aɷəz 'leɪtə ðə 'sɛvn̩ 'skaɷts keɪm 'bak ən 'sɛd, 'wi v 'faɷnd
ə 'stoɷn 'haɷs wɪtʃ ɪz 'dʒʌst wɒt wi 'wɒntɪd: ðə z 'rum ən 'gɒd
'fud fər əs 'əl. ðə z ə 'kaɪndlɪ 'hɒs neɪmd 'nɛlɪ, ə 'kaɷ, ə 'kaf, ənd
ə 'gadn̩ wɪð ən 'ɛlm tri.' 'dʒʌst 'ðɛn ði 'oɷld 'rat kət 'saɪt əv jʌŋ
'aθə. 'ə 'ju kʌmɪŋ 'wɪð əs?' hi askt. 'aɪ 'doɷnt 'noɷ,' aθə saɪd,
'ðə 'ruf 'meɪ nɒt kʌm 'daɷn dʒʌst 'jɛt.' "wɛl,' sɛd ði 'oɷld 'rat
'aŋgrɪlɪ, 'wi 'kant 'weɪt əl 'deɪ fə jɷ tə 'meɪk ʌp jɷ 'maɪnd. 'raɪt
əbaɷt 'feɪs! 'matʃ!' ən ðeɪ 'wɛnt 'ɒf.

'aθə 'stɒd ən 'wɒtʃt ði 'ʌðə rats 'hʌrɪ ə'weɪ. ði aɪ'dɪə əv ən
ɪ'mɪdʒət dɪ'sɪʒn̩ wəz 'tu 'mʌtʃ fər ɪm. 'aɪl goɷ 'bak tə maɪ 'hoɷl
fər ə bɪt,' hi 'sɛd tɷ ɪm'sɛlf, "dʒʌst tə 'meɪk ʌp maɪ 'maɪnd.'

'ðat 'naɪt ðə wəz ə 'greɪt 'kraʃ ðət 'ʃɒk ði 'ɜθ, ən 'daɷn keɪm
ðə 'hoɷl 'ruf. 'nɛkst 'deɪ səm 'mɛn roɷd ʌp ən 'lɒkt ət ðə 'rɔɪnz.
'wʌn əv ðəm 'muvd ə 'bɒd, ənd 'ʌndər ɪt ðeɪ sɔ ə 'jʌŋ 'rat laɪɪŋ
ɒn ɪz 'saɪd, 'kwaɪt 'dɛd, 'haf 'ɪn ən 'haf 'aɷt əv ɪz 'hoɷl.

After HENRY SWEET, 1890

# 16. ðə ˈnəθ ˈwɪnd ən ðə ˈsʌn

ðə ˈnəθ ˈwɪnd ən ðə ˈsʌn wə dɪsˈpjutɪŋ ˈwɪtʃ wəz ðə ˈstrɒŋgə, wɛn ə ˈtravlə keɪm əˈlɒŋ ˈrapt ɪn ə ˈwəm ˈkloʊk. ðeɪ əˈgrid ðət ðə ˈwʌn hu ˈfəst səkˈsidɪd ɪn ˈmeɪkɪŋ ðə ˈtravlə teɪk ɪz ˈkloʊk ɒf ʃʊd bɪ kənˈsɪdəd ˈstrɒŋgə ðən ðɪ ˈʌðə. ˈðɛn ðə ˈnəθ ˈwɪnd ˈblu əz ˈhɑd əz i ˈkʊd, bət ðə ˈmər i ˈblu ðə mə ˈkloʊslɪ dɪd ðə ˈtravlə ˈfoʊld ɪz ˈkloʊk əˈraʊnd ɪm; ənd ət ˈlɑst ðə ˈnəθ ˈwɪnd ˈgeɪv ʌp ði əˈtɛmpt. ˈðɛn ðə ˈsʌn ˈʃɒn aʊt ˈwəmlɪ, ənd ɪˈmidʒətlɪ ðə ˈtravlə ˈtʊk əf ɪz ˈkloʊk. ən ˈsoʊ ðə ˈnəθ ˈwɪnd wəz əˈblaɪdʒd tə kənˈfɛs ðət ðə ˈsʌn wəz ðə ˈstrɒŋgər əv ðə ˈtu.

'ðoꞷz hu 'hav ət 'taɪmz 'faꞷnd ɪt 'nɛsəsrɪ, fə 'wʌn rizn̩ ər
ə'nʌðə, tə prə'djus ə 'spɛsɪmɪn 'tɛkst ɪn fə'nɛtɪk trans'krɪpʃən wɪl
əv ɪks'pɪərɪənst ə 'dɪfɪkḷtɪ ɪn sə'lɛktɪŋ ə 'sutəbḷ 'pasɪdʒ. tə bi
aɪ'dɪəlɪ 'sutəbḷ ɪt ʃəd fꞷlfɪl 'fə rɪ'kwaɪəmənts. ɪt ʃꞷd
   ('wʌn) kəntein 'ɔl ðə 'sɪmbḷz,
   ('tu) ɪg'zɛmplɪfaɪ ðə 'tʃif fɪ'nɒmɪnə əv 'wiknɪŋ, 'ʃətnɪŋ, 'strɛs,
'wɜd-lɪŋkɪŋ, ɪt'sɛtrə,
   ('θri) meɪk 'sɛns,
   ('fə) bi əz 'ʃɔt əz 'pɒsəbḷ.
naꞷ 'ɪf wi sə'lɛkt ə 'pasɪdʒ ət 'randəm frəm 'ɛnɪ 'bꞷk, bɪ'fər
aꞷə kən'dɪʃn̩z 'wʌn, 'tu ən 'θri ə fꞷl'fɪld, ðə 'tɛkst 'dʌznt fꞷlfɪl
kən'dɪʃn̩ 'fə. ɒn ði 'ʌðə hand, ɪf wi rɪs'trɪkt aꞷə 'pasɪdʒ ɪn 'ədə fər
ɪt tə kən'fəm tə kən'dɪʃn̩ 'fə ɪt wɪl 'nɒt fꞷlfɪl kən'dɪʃn̩z 'wʌn, 'tu
ən 'θri.
  ðə 'fɒloꞷɪŋ 'pasɪdʒ ɪz ən 'ɛseɪ tədz 'faɪndɪŋ ə 'tɛkst wɪtʃ ðə
moꞷst 'nɪəlɪ fꞷl'fɪlz ðə 'fə rɪ'kwaɪəmənts.

ət 'wɒt 'taɪm ə jꞷ 'goꞷɪŋ tə ði ɛksɪ'bɪʃn̩? aɪ 'θɔt aɪ 'hɜd jꞷ 'tɛl
jə 'brʌðə ðɪs 'mənɪŋ ðət jꞷ ɪks'pɛktɪd tə 'mit ɪm 'ðɛər ət əbaꞷt 'tu.
'jɛs. wɒd 'ju laɪk tə 'dʒɔɪn əs ðɛə?
  aɪ 'wꞷd, wɪð 'plɛʒə, bət aɪ m 'nɒt 'ʃꞷə weðər aɪ 'kan. ɪn 'ɛnɪ
keɪs aɪ məst 'liv 'ɜlɪ tə 'katʃ ðə 'fə 'treɪn. aɪ 'doꞷnt 'lɪv hɪə 'naꞷ; aɪ
'lɪv ɪn ðə 'sʌbɜbz, ənd aɪ 'wɒnt tə gɛt 'hoꞷm bɪfər ɪts 'dɑk.
  'ɑ jꞷ 'rɪəlɪ ɪn sʌtʃ ə 'hʌrɪ tə gɛt 'hoꞷm? 'mʌst jꞷ? ɪf ɪts 'soꞷlɪ
ɒn 'ðat ə'kaꞷnt, wi kən 'teɪk jꞷ 'bak ɪn aꞷə 'kɑ.
  'kan jꞷ? 'ðat ḷ bɪ 'splɛndɪd. 'ɔl 'raɪt.
H. E. Palmer, 1925

# Other Types of Transcription

To illustrate the range of variation in types of transcription which have been used for RP, a representative selection of specimens is given in this Appendix. The passage which has been transcribed is the same in each case—the 'model English phonetic text' devised by H. E. Palmer (see above, p. 67). Only types of transcription which use the symbols, and follow the traditions, of the IPA are included among the specimens. RP has, of course, often been transcribed in other phonetic alphabets, but specimens of these would not be to the point here—the point being that the same passage, spoken in the same pronunciation, may always legitimately be transcribed in more than one way in any system of phonetic notation. Each way may have, for certain purposes, its own peculiar advantages (and, for other purposes, disadvantages): in other words, there is no one, true transcription of a language.

One should remember, in evaluating these specimens, that the traditions of the phonetic transcription of English go back a long way. They go back to well before the founding of the IPA (which was in 1886)—through Henry Sweet, A. J. Ellis, A. M. Bell and Isaac Pitman to Thomas Batchelor and others at the very beginning of the nineteenth century. The evolution of the different types of transcription in use today has been governed by various factors, not the least of which has been the inertia of published texts: a radical departure from tradition has seldom proved popular. The great number of books, and especially books by Daniel Jones, which use the type known familiarly as 'EPD' transcription (after the initials of Jones's *English*

69

*Pronouncing Dictionary*: the type is illustrated in Specimen IV)
have served to perpetuate a way of representing RP which is,
for many purposes, an unsatisfactory one. Specimen VI, on
the other hand, illustrates an excellent type of transcription,
with many possible applications, which has been undeservedly
neglected—perhaps because it conforms with unwonted strict-
ness to IPA principles. However, in spite of the weight of tradition, a very large number of types of IPA transcription of RP
have by now seen print (many more, as a matter of fact, than are
illustrated in the following specimens).

These different types of transcription do not show much
variation in their treatment of consonants, which for the most
part is simple phonemic. They differ from each other most
strikingly in their degree of 'symbol-economy' in the representation of vowels, that is to say in the number of different letters
used, and in their distribution over the items to be represented.
The variation arises chiefly from different decisions being made
on two points: whether to adopt a qualitative or a quantitative
basis for the representation of monophthongs; and whether to
adopt a phonemic or an allophonic treatment of the first elements
of diphthongs. There are three areas in the RP vowel-system
where this variation in symbol-economy is particularly marked,
and these areas are perhaps worth looking at in some detail
before the specimen texts are given.

The first of these areas comprises four items: the two monophthongs in the words *bet* and *bat*, and the first elements (only) of
the two diphthongs in the words *bait* and *bare*. To cover this
range of items, some types of transcription have used two different letters, some have used three, and some four. Table One,
below, illustrates the various possibilities. A type of transcription
that uses only two different letters will be, in this area at least, a
phonemic transcription. Two equally valid phonemic interpretations are possible here. In the first, each of the two letters
represents two items, a monophthong and the first element of a
diphthong; column 5 of Table One exhibits this arrangement. In
the second, one letter represents three items, a monophthong and
both first elements of the diphthongs, while the other represents

the remaining monophthong only; column 6 exhibits this other distribution. Types of transcription which use more than two different letters to cover this area will be allophonic, and there are several possibilities here, all of which can be found in published texts. Four different letters can be used, one for each item, as shown in column 1 of Table One. If three different letters are used, they can be arranged to cover the items in three ways, and the remaining columns of the Table show these three other distributions.

The following table, then, shows how four, three or two different letters can be used to cover the four items shown at the left-hand side. (The second elements of the diphthongs are ignored for the present purpose.) The actual shapes of the various letters are, of course, immaterial, the point of the table being the number of different letters contained in each column, and the way the letters are distributed over the four items.

| | 1 | 2 | 3 | 4 | 5 | 6 |
|---|---|---|---|---|---|---|
| *bait* (first element) | e | e | e | e | e | e |
| *bet* | ę | e | ɛ | ɛ | e | e |
| *bare* (first element) | ɛ | ɛ | ɛ | æ | ɛ | e |
| *bat* | æ | æ | a | æ | ɛ | a |

TABLE ONE

The following are some of the published texts in which the distributions shown in columns 1 to 6 have appeared:

1  R. Grant Brown, 1953. (Four letters are also used by B. Dumville, 1909, though one of them is not an authorized IPA symbol.)

2  D. Jones, *English Pronouncing Dictionary*, and many other works by Jones and by other writers (see Specimen IV).

3  D. Jones, *The Pronunciation of English* (3rd and 4th editions), and various other types of transcription including that used in the present book (see Specimens III and V).

4  Mackenzie and Drew (1919).

5  W. Jassem (1952 and other works; see Specimen VII).

6  D. Jones, *The Phoneme*, works by P. A. D. MacCarthy and others, and various other types of transcription (see Specimens I, II, VI and VIII).

The second area of variation overlaps slightly with the first. It comprises five items, the three monophthongs in the words *bat*, *bath* and *but*, and the first elements of the diphthongs in the words *bite* and *bout*. Again, as many as four, or as few as two, different letters can be used to cover this range of five items, and in addition the letters can be distributed in various ways over the items. Some (though not all) of the possibilities here are shown in Table Two. (As before, the second elements of diphthongs are ignored, and so in this Table is the possible presence of a length-mark.)

|  | 1 | 2 | 3 | 4 | 5 | 6 | 7 |
|---|---|---|---|---|---|---|---|
| *bat* | æ | æ | a | ɛ | a |  | æ |
| *bath* | ɑ | ɑ |  | ɑ | ɑ | a |  |
| *bout* (first element) |  | a | ɑ |  | a |  | a |
| *bite* (first element) | a |  |  | a |  |  |  |
| *but* | ʌ | ʌ | ʌ |  | ʌ | ʌ |  |

TABLE TWO

# Other types of transcription

The distributions shown in columns 1 to 7 have been used as follows:

1 D. Jones, *The Pronunciation of English* (1st and 2nd editions).
2 D. Jones, *English Pronouncing Dictionary*, and various other types of transcription (see Specimens IV and V).
3 D. Jones, *The Pronunciation of English* (3rd and 4th editions), and some other types (see Specimens III and VI).
4 W. Jassem (see Specimen VII).
5 The type of transcription used in the present book (note that there are only three different letters in this distribution, one of them appearing twice in the column).
6 Works by P. A. D. MacCarthy and others (see Specimens I and II).
7 See Specimen VIII.

The third area of variation is illustrated in Table Three below; it comprises four items, the three monophthongs in the words *nought*, *not*, *hurt* and the first element of the diphthong in the word *note*. Two, three or four letters can be used to cover this range. (The second element of the diphthong, and the possible presence of a length-mark, are ignored.)

|  | 1 | 2 | 3 | 4 | 5 | 6 |
|---|---|---|---|---|---|---|
| *nought* | ɔ | ɔ | ɔ | o | ɔ | o |
| *not* | ɒ |  | o | ɔ |  |  |
| *note* (first element) | o | o |  | 3 | ə | ə |
| *hurt* | 3 | ə | ə |  |  |  |

TABLE THREE

The distributions shown in columns 1 to 6 have been used as follows:

1   The type of transcription used in the present book, and the type used in works by Miss Lilias E. Armstrong and Miss Ida C. Ward (see Specimen V).
2   D. Jones, *The Pronunciation of English* and *English Pronouncing Dictionary* (see Specimens III and IV).
3   H. Sweet, *The Sounds of English* (this type of transcription does not, in some other respects, agree with IPA principles).
4   See Specimens VI and VII.
5   See Specimen VIII.
6   Works by P. A. D. MacCarthy and others (see Specimens I and II).

The specimens follow. Each specimen is accompanied by a few brief notes on the history of the type of transcription which it illustrates, and on the use that has been made of it. The notes also characterize the type of transcription by distinguishing it as either (*a*) simple or comparative; (*b*) phonemic or allophonic as regards the first elements of diphthongs; (*c*) phonemic or allophonic in other respects; (*d*) qualitative or quantitative in the representation of monophthongs; and (*e*) vocalic or consonantal in the treatment of second elements of diphthongs. A list is given of the different vowel letters used in the transcription. In order to facilitate the comparison of specimens with each other, the lines of the text are numbered, and so arranged that they correspond exactly in each version.

# SPECIMEN I

This type of transcription is sometimes called 'simplified' or 'extra-broad'. It has been used by N. C. Scott, *English Conversations in Simplified Phonetic Transcription* (1942), E. L. Tibbitts, *A Phonetic Reader for Foreign Learners of English* (1946), and is to be found in an increasing number of other books. It was devised by Daniel Jones, and first made public by him in 1931 (see *Le Maître Phonétique*, 1931, p. 12). Jones himself uses it in *The Phoneme* (1950). It is a type which attains the maximum symbol-economy possible in an IPA transcription of English. The type of transcription illustrated in Specimen II is closely similar to this one.

The transcription is

(*a*) simple,
(*b*), (*c*) phonemic in all respects,
(*d*) quantitative in representation of monophthongs,
(*e*) vocalic in representation of second elements of diphthongs.

The total number of different vowel letters is seven, viz.

a   e   i   o   u   ʌ   ə

The length-mark is an additional sign.

# SPECIMEN I

1      ət 'wot 'taim ə ju 'gouiŋ tə ði: eksi'biʃn̩?
2   ai 'θo:t ai 'hə:d ju 'tel jo: 'brʌðə ðis 'mo:niŋ
3   ðət ju iks'pektid tə 'mi:t im 'ðeər ət əbaut 'tu:.
4      'jes. wud 'ju: laik tə 'dʒoin əs ðeə?
5      ai 'wud, wið 'pleʒə, bət ai m 'not 'ʃuə weðer
6   ai 'kan. in 'eni keis ai məst 'li:v 'ə:li tə
7   'katʃ ðə 'fo: 'trein. ai 'dount 'liv hiə 'nau;
8   ai 'liv in ðə 'sʌbə:bz ənd ai 'wont tə get 'houm
9   bifo:r its 'da:k.
10    'a: ju 'riəli in sʌtʃ ə 'hʌri tə get 'houm?
11   'mʌst ju? if its 'soulli on 'ðat ə'kaunt, wi:
12   kən 'teik ju 'bak in auə 'ka:.
13   'kan ju? 'ðat l̩ bi 'splendid! 'o:l 'rait.

'sʌbə:bz

# SPECIMEN II

This type of transcription is a modification of the so-called 'simplified' or 'extra-broad' type shown in Specimen I. It was devised by P. A. D. MacCarthy, and is used in his *English Pronunciation* (1944), *English Pronouncing Vocabulary* (1945), and *English Conversation Reader* (1956). The modification consists of dispensing with the length-mark, and instead indicating long vowels by doubling the vowel letter (this practice does not, strictly speaking, conform to IPA principles, according to which a doubled symbol implies two syllables). In other respects the transcription is the same as in the preceding specimen. This one modification, however, makes a considerable difference to the general effect of the text.

The transcription, like Specimen I, is

- (*a*) simple,
- (*b*), (*c*) phonemic in all respects,
- (*d*) quantitative in representation of monophthongs,
- (*e*) vocalic in representation of second elements of diphthongs.

The total number of different vowel letters is seven, viz.

a  e  i  o  u  ʌ  ə

# SPECIMEN II

1     ət 'wot 'taim ə ju 'gouiŋ tə ðii eksi'biʃn̩?

2    ai 'θoot ai 'həəd ju 'tel joo 'brʌðə ðis 'mooniŋ

3    ðet ju iks'pektid tə 'miit im 'ðeər ət əbaut 'tuu.

4     'jes. wud 'ju laik tə 'dʒoin əs ðeə?

5    ai 'wud, wið 'pleʒə, bət ai m 'not 'ʃuə weðər

6    ai 'kan. in 'eni keis ai məst 'liiv 'əəli tə

7    'katʃ ðə 'foo 'trein. ai 'dount 'liv hiə 'nau;

8    ai 'liv in ðə 'sʌbəəbz ənd ai 'wont tə get 'houm

9    bifoor its 'daak.

10     'aa ju 'riəli in sʌtʃ ə 'hʌri tə get 'houm?

11    'mʌst ju? if its 'soulli on 'ðat ə'kaunt, wii

12    kən 'teik ju 'bak in auə 'kaa.

13     'kan ju? 'ðat l̩ bi 'splendid! 'ool 'rait.

# SPECIMEN III

This type of transcription is used in Daniel Jones's *Pronunciation of English* in its third and fourth editions (1950 and 1956). (The earlier editions used the type shown in Specimen IV, with one small difference—[ɑu] for [au].) It is also used in *Specimens of English in Phonetic Transcription* by M. Chapallaz, where it is described as 'slightly "narrow" '.

The transcription is

(*a*) simple,
(*b*) allophonic as regards the first elements of the diphthongs [ei, ou],
(*c*) allophonic in distinguishing [a] and [ɑ],
(*d*) quantitative in representation of some monophthongs, though [a] and [ɑː] are not paired,
(*e*) vocalic in representation of second elements of diphthongs.

The total number of different vowel letters is ten, viz.

a  e  i  o  u  ɑ  ɛ  ɒ  ʌ  ə

# SPECIMEN III

1    ət 'wɔt 'taim ə ju 'gouiŋ tə ði: ɛksi'biʃn?
2    ai 'θɔːt ai 'hɜːd ju 'tɛl jɔː 'brʌðə ðis 'mɔːniŋ
3    ðət ju iks'pɛktid tə 'miːt im 'ðɛər ət əbaut 'tuː.
4    'jɛs. wud 'ju laik tə 'dʒɔin əs ðɛə?
5    ai 'wud, wið 'plɛʒə, bət aim 'nɔt 'ʃuə wɛðər
6    ai 'kan. in 'ɛni keis ai məst 'liːv 'ɜːli tə
7    'katʃ ðə 'fɔː 'trein. ai 'dount 'liv hiə 'nau;
8    ai 'liv in ðə 'sʌbəːbz ənd ai 'wɔnt tə gɛt 'houm
9    bifɔːr its 'daːk.
10    'aː ju 'riəli in sʌtʃ ə 'hʌri tə gɛt 'houm?
11    'mʌst ju? if its 'soulli ɔn 'ðat ə'kaunt, wiː
12    kən 'teik ju 'bak in auə 'kaː.
13    'kan ju? 'ðat l̩ bi 'splɛndid! 'ɔːl 'rait.

# SPECIMEN IV

This is the type of transcription used in three of Daniel Jones's most influential books: *Phonetic Readings in English* (1912, etc.), *English Pronouncing Dictionary* (1917, etc.), and *Outline of English Phonetics* (1918, etc.). It is often, and very conveniently, called 'EPD' transcription, after the initials of the second of these books. It is also sometimes referred to as 'the Jones transcription', although it was not invented by Daniel Jones, as this name would seem to imply—it was the type of transcription of English generally (though not exclusively) employed by contributors to the *Maître Phonétique* when Jones, in 1905, joined the IPA. This type of transcription has never, in any sense, been an official IPA transcription of English, though it is sometimes called 'the IPA broad transcription' (there is no official IPA transcription of any language). Jones himself has used other types of transcription in *The Phoneme* (see Specimen I above), and in recent editions of *The Pronunciation of English* (see Specimen III above). 'EPD' transcription has been used in books and articles by very many other writers.

The transcription is

    (*a*) simple,

    (*b*) allophonic as regards the first elements of the diphthongs [ai, au, ɛə, ou],

    (*c*) allophonic in distinguishing [æ] and [ɑ],

    (*d*) quantitative in representation of monophthongs,

    (*e*) vocalic in representation of the second elements of diphthongs.

The total number of different vowel letters is eleven, viz.

a  e  i  o  u  æ  ɑ  ɛ  ɔ  ʌ  ə

The length-mark is an additional sign.

# SPECIMEN IV

1     ət 'wɒt 'taim ə ju 'gouiŋ tə ði: eksi'biʃn̩?
2   ai 'θɔ:t ai 'hə:d ju 'tel jɔ: 'brʌðə ðis 'mɔ:niŋ
3   ðət ju iks'pektid tə 'mi:t im 'ðɛər ət əbaut 'tu:.
4     'jes. wud 'ju: laik tə 'dʒɔin əs ðɛə?
5     ai 'wud, wið 'pleʒə, bət ai m 'nɒt 'ʃuə weðər
6   ai 'kæn. in 'eni keis ai məst 'li:v 'ə:li tə
7   'kætʃ ðə 'fɔ: 'trein. ai 'dount 'liv hiə 'nau;
8   ai 'liv in ðə 'sʌbə:bz ənd ai 'wənt tə get 'houm
9   bifɔ:r its 'da:k.
10     'a: ju 'riəli in sʌtʃ ə 'hʌri tə get 'houm?
11   'mʌst ju? if its 'soulli ɒn 'ðæt ə'kaunt, wi:
12   kən 'teik ju 'bæk in auə 'ka:.
13   'kæn ju? 'ðæt l̩ bi 'splendid! 'ɔ:l 'rait.

'sʌbə:bz    suburbs

mɔ:niŋ    morning

ə:li    early

bifɔ:r    before

hə:d    heard

brʌðə    brother

ʃuə    sure

# SPECIMEN V

Lilias E. Armstrong, at the request of Daniel Jones, prepared, and published in 1923, *An English Phonetic Reader* in which the type of transcription shown in this specimen was used. It is basically a qualitative transcription in its representation of monophthongs, but it also gives indications of vowel length. It is a type which has proved very popular, and it has been used by a number of writers in their books and articles, and notably by Ida C. Ward in *Defects of Speech* and *The Phonetics of English*, and L. E. Armstrong and I. C. Ward, *A Handbook of English Intonation*. It is sometimes called 'the IPA narrow transcription'.

A mark for 'half-length', as well as the usual length-mark, is used, and allophones of vowels of three degrees of duration can thus be distinguished: compare [jɔ] (line 2), [θɚ·t] (line 2) and [fɔː] (line 7); but in the above works these allophones are only distinguished in the case of [i ɑ ɔ u ɜ], and not in the case of the remaining vowels. (In the accompanying text the more recent IPA letter [ɷ] has been used in place of the older [ʊ] which appears in the books mentioned above.)

The transcription is

(*a*) simple,

(*b*) allophonic as regards the first elements of the diphthongs [aɪ aɷ eɪ oɷ],

(*c*) allophonic also in the indications of vowel duration,

(*d*) qualitative in representation of monophthongs,

(*e*) vocalic in representation of second elements of diph-thongs.

The total number of different vowel letters is fifteen, viz.

a e i o u æ ɑ ɒ ɛ ɜ ə ɪ ɔ ɷ ʌ

The length-mark and the half-length-mark are additional signs.

# SPECIMEN V

1    ət 'wɒt 'taɪm ə jɷ 'goɷɪŋ tə ði ɛksɪ'bɪʃn̩?
2    aɪ 'θɚt aɪ 'hɜˑd jɷ 'tɛl jɔ 'brʌðə ðɪs 'mɔˑnɪŋ
3    ðət jɷ ɪks'pɛktɪd tə 'miˑt ɪm 'ðɛər ət əbaɷt 'tuː.
4    'jɛs. wɷd 'juː laɪk tə 'dʒɔɪn əs ðɛə?
5    aɪ 'wɷd, wɪð 'plɛʒə, bət aɪm 'nɒt 'ʃɷə wɛðər
6    aɪ 'kæn. ɪn 'ɛnɪ keɪs aɪ məst 'liːv 'ɜːlɪ tə
7    'kætʃ ðə 'fɔː 'treɪn. aɪ 'doɷnt 'lɪv hɪə 'naɷ;
8    aɪ 'lɪv ɪn ðə 'sʌbɜːbz ənd aɪ 'wɒnt tə gɛt 'hoɷm
9    bɪfər ɪts 'dɑˑk.
10   'ɑˑ jɷ 'rɪəlɪ ɪn sʌtʃ ə 'hʌrɪ tə gɛt 'hoɷm?
11   'mʌst jɷ? ɪf ɪts 'soɷlɪ ɒn 'ðæt ə'kaɷnt, wi
12   kən 'teɪk jɷ 'bæk ɪn aɷə 'kɑː.
13   'kæn jɷ? 'ðæt l̩ bɪ 'splɛndɪd! 'ɔːl 'raɪt.

# SPECIMEN VI

This type of transcription is included more as a curiosity than anything else; it has not been used to any extent in published texts. Nevertheless it is possibly more strictly in accordance with IPA principles than any other type of transcription of English so far put forward. It derives from proposals made by Paul Passy in the *Maître Phonétique* (1926, p. 14, and 1932, p. 50), and it follows rigorously the principle of using the symbol of the nearest Cardinal Vowel for the monophthongs (see IPA, *Principles*, 1949, p. 7). It thus presents a radical departure from the general tradition of English transcriptions, especially in the representation of the vowels in *with* and *would*. The nearest Cardinal Vowels to these are Two and Seven respectively, and the words therefore appear in this specimen as [weð] and [wod]. The transcription can thus be qualitative in representation of monophthongs, and yet avoid the rather unsatisfactory letters (typographically speaking) [ɪ] and [ʊ]. It might, for this and other reasons, have many advantages for teaching purposes.

Although the effect is so very different from other transcriptions of English, it is worth noting that the IPA transcription traditionally used for Danish uses [e] and [o] for vowels very similar to those of English *with* and *would* (see H. J. Uldall, 1933).

The transcription is

    (*a*) simple,
    (*b*), (*c*) phonemic in all respects,
    (*d*) qualitative in representation of monophthongs,
    (*e*) vocalic in representation of second elements of diphthongs.

The total number of different vowel letters is twelve, viz.

a e i o u ɑ ɒ ɛ ɔ ʌ ɜ ə

# SPECIMEN VI

1    ət 'wɒt 'taem ə jo 'gɜoeŋ tə ði ɛkse'beʃn̩?
2    ae 'θət ae 'hɜd jo 'tɛl jə 'brʌðə ðes 'məneŋ
3    ðət jo eks'pɛkted tə 'mit em 'ðɛər ət əbaot 'tu.
4    'jɛs. wod 'ju laek tə 'dʒɒen əs ðɛə?
5    ae 'wod, weð 'plɛʒə, bət aem 'nɒt 'ʃoə wɛðər
6    ae 'kan. en 'ɛne kɛes ae məst 'liv 'ɜle tə
7    'katʃ ðə 'fə 'trɛen. ae 'dɜont 'lev heə 'nao;
8    ae 'lev en ðə 'sʌbɜbz ənd ae 'wɒnt tə gɛt 'hɜom
9    befər ets 'dɑk.
10   'ɑ jo 'reəle en sʌtʃ ə 'hʌre tə gɛt 'hɜom?
11   'mʌst jo? ef ets 'sɜolle ɒn 'ðat ə'kaont, wi
12   kən 'tɛek jo 'bak en aoə 'kɑ.
13   'kan jo? 'ðat l̩ be 'splɛnded! 'ɔl 'rɑet.

# SPECIMEN VII

This type of transcription is used by Wiktor Jassem in his *Intonation of Conversational English* (1952), and other works. It is only slightly different from a type proposed by A. C. Lawrenson in the *Maître Phonétique* (1935), and a number of other types have closely resembled it.

Characteristic features of this transcription, and others of similar type, are the treatment of the vowels in the words *meet* and *two* as diphthongs and not monophthongs; and the consonantal representation of the second elements of these diphthongs, together with those in the words *case, time, join, go, about*. Although most of the types of transcription used for RP have probably been vocalic in their representation of second elements of diphthongs, there is a very long tradition behind the consonantal representation: it goes back at least as far as Thomas Batchelor (see p. 58 of his *Orthoëpical Analysis*, 1809). It seems to have been first proposed for IPA transcriptions by Alfred D. Schoch (1907). Many subsequent writers have adopted it, particularly L. Bloomfield (1935) and G. L. Trager (1935).

The transcription is

(*a*) simple,
(*b*), (*c*) phonemic in all respects,
(*d*) qualitative in representation of monophthongs,
(*e*) consonantal in representation of second elements of diphthongs.

The total number of different vowel letters is ten, viz.

a  e  i  o  u  ɑ  ɛ  ɔ  ɜ  ə

# SPECIMEN VII

1     ət 'wɒt 'tajm ə ju 'gɜwiŋ tə ðij eksi'biʃn̩?
2   aj 'θot aj 'hɜd ju 'tel jo 'braðə ðis 'moniŋ
3   ðət ju iks'pektid tə 'mijt im 'ðɛər ət əbawt 'tuw.
4     'jes. wud 'juw lajk tə 'dʒɔjn əs ðɛə?
5     aj 'wud, wið 'pleʒə, bət ajm 'nɒt 'ʃuə weðər
6   aj 'kɛn. in 'eni kejs aj məst 'lijv 'ɜli tə
7   'kɛtʃ ðə 'fo 'trejn. aj 'dɜwnt 'liv hiə 'naw;
8   aj 'liv in ðə 'sabɜbz ənd aj 'wɒnt tə get 'hɜwm
9   bifor its 'dɑk.
10     'ɑ ju 'riəli in satʃ ə 'hari tə get 'hɜwm?
11   'mast ju? if its 'sɜwlli ɒn 'ðɛt ə'kawnt, wij
12   kən 'tejk ju 'bɛk in awə 'kɑ.
13     'kɛn ju? 'ðɛt ļ bi 'splendid. 'ol 'rajt.

# SPECIMEN VIII

The consonantal treatment of second elements of diphthongs can be carried farther than is done in Specimen VII: it can also, as the present transcription illustrates, be applied to the diphthongs in the words *here*, *there*, and *sure*. The second element of these diphthongs can be regarded as being in complementary distribution with the consonant [h], and it can therefore be transcribed with the same symbol. Moreover the vowels in the words *dark*, *thought*, and *early* may also be looked on as diphthongs with [h] as second element (just as those in *meet* and *two* can be looked on as diphthongs with [j] and [w] as second elements). (See G. L. Trager and B. Bloch, 1941.) The number of vowels treated as monophthongs is thus greatly reduced, making considerable symbol-economy possible without having recourse to a quantitative treatment. Although this approach has recently proved very popular for other types of English, it has not so far been used to any great extent for transcribing RP.

The transcription is

> (*a*) comparative (the letter [o] is not used, though it would be in transcribing other kinds of English in this system),
> (*b*), (*c*) phonemic in all respects,
> (*d*) qualitative in representation of monophthongs,
> (*e*) consonantal in representation of second elements of diphthongs.

The total number of different vowel letters is seven, viz.

a  e  i  u  æ  ɔ  ə

# SPECIMEN VIII

1     ət 'wɔt 'tajm ə ju 'gəwiŋ tə ðij eksi'biʃən?
2     aj 'θɔht aj 'həhd ju 'tel jɔh 'braðə ðis 'məhniŋ
3     ðət juw iks'pektid tə 'mijt im 'ðehr ət əbawt 'tuw.
4     'jes. wud 'juw lajk tə 'dʒɔjn əs ðeh?
5     aj 'wud, wið 'pleʒə, bət aj m 'nɔt 'ʃuh weðər
6     aj 'kæn. in 'eni kejs aj məst 'lijv 'əhli tə
7     'kætʃ ðə 'fəh 'trejn. aj 'dəwnt 'liv hih 'naw;
8     aj 'liv in ðə 'sabəhbz ənd aj 'wɔnt tə get 'həwm
9     bifəhr its 'dahk.
10    'ah ju 'rihli in satʃ ə 'hari tə get 'həwm?
11    'məst ju? if its 'səwlli ɔn 'ðæt ə'kawnt, wij
12    kən 'tejk ju 'bæk in awə 'kah.
13    'kæn ju? 'ðæt əl bi 'splendid! 'əhl 'rajt.

## Appendix I

The following table makes it possible to compare at a glance the way in which the RP vowels are represented in the eight types of transcription illustrated in this Appendix. It will be seen that no. 12 is the only vowel which receives the same symbol in all eight types.

| | | I | II | III | IV | V | VI | VII | VIII |
|---|---|---|---|---|---|---|---|---|---|
| 1 | bead | iː | ii | iː | iː | i | i | ij | ij |
| 2 | bid | i | i | i | i | ɪ | e | i | i |
| 3 | bed | e | e | ɛ | e | ɛ | ɛ | e | e |
| 4 | bad | a | a | a | æ | æ | a | ɛ | æ |
| 5 | bard | aː | aa | ɑː | ɑː | ɑ | ɑ | ɑ | ah |
| 6 | bog | o | o | ɔ | ɔ | ɒ | ɒ | ɔ | ɔ |
| 7 | board | ɔː | oo | ɔː | ɔː | ɔ | ɔ | o | ɔh |
| 8 | good | u | u | u | u | ꭒ | o | u | u |
| 9 | food | uː | uu | uː | uː | u | u | uw | uw |
| 10 | bud | ʌ | ʌ | ʌ | ʌ | ʌ | ʌ | a | a |
| 11 | bird | ɔː | əə | ɔː | ɔː | 3 | 3 | 3 | ɔh |
| 12 | about | ə | ə | ə | ə | ə | ə | ə | ə |
| 13 | day | ei | ei | ei | ei | eɪ | ɛe | ej | ej |
| 14 | no | ou | ou | ou | ou | oꭒ | 3o | 3w | ɔw |
| 15 | eye | ai | ai | ɑi | ai | aɪ | ɑe | aj | aj |
| 16 | now | au | au | ɑu | au | aꭒ | ɑo | aw | aw |
| 17 | boy | oi | oi | ɔi | ɔi | ɔɪ | ɒe | ɔj | ɔj |
| 18 | beer | iə | iə | iə | iə | ɪə | eə | iə | ih |
| 19 | bare | eə | eə | ɛə | ɛə | ɛə | ɛə | ɛə | eh |
| 20 | poor | uə | uə | uə | uə | ꭒə | oə | uə | uh |

# Orthographic Versions

## 1. Language

Language—human speech—is an inexhaustible abundance of manifold treasures. Language is inseparable from man and follows him in all his works. Language is the instrument with which man forms thought and feeling, mood, aspiration, will and act, the instrument by whose means he influences and is influenced, the ultimate and deepest foundation of human society. But it is also the ultimate, indispensable sustainer of the human individual, his refuge in hours of loneliness, when the mind wrestles with existence and the conflict is resolved in the monologue of the poet and the thinker. Before the first awakening of our consciousness language was echoing about us, ready to close around our first tender seed of thought and to accompany us inseparably through life, from the simple activities of everyday living to our most sublime and intimate moments—those moments from which we borrow warmth and strength for our daily life through that hold of memory that language itself gives us. But language is no external accompaniment. It lies deep in the mind of man, a wealth of memories inherited by the individual and the tribe, a vigilant conscience that reminds and warns. And speech is the distinctive mark of the personality, for good and ill, the distinctive mark of home and of nation, mankind's patent of nobility. So inextricably has language grown inside personality, home, nation, mankind, and life itself that we may sometimes be tempted to ask whether language is a mere reflexion of, or simply *is* not all those things—the very seed leaf of their growth.

Louis Hjelmslev, *Prolegomena to a Theory of Language*, 1953, Ch. 1, translated by Francis J. Whitfield from the Danish *Omkring sprogteoriens grundlæggelse*, 1943.

# 2. Control of Language

Apparently we suppose that the 'gift' of language is like the 'gift' of a nose, entirely (as to its position and office) outside the scope of our modifying control. And it is true that we cannot invert our nose, or give it four nostrils, or present it with the power of hearing or sight. Neither, indeed, can we develop it into an organ of (at present) transcendent smell, no, nor even restore to it its pristine and sub-human privileges. But all this only shows that we had better leave off talking of 'gift' when speaking of language. Rather, we have painfully earned the possession of speech by learning to control and order the sounds producible by our evolving larynx, and by continuously, consistently, arduously, purposively developing the complexities of the resulting system of vocal signs. In doing this we have evolved and developed syntax and prosody and much else that the philologist, orator, or poet can expound to us, or use to influence our feeling and action. The point is, that just when the need of adding consensus to a so far accomplished control was most urgent, and its neglect most certain to be disastrous to our intellectual fortunes; just when a high civilisation and what we call the modern era of discovery and its reaction on philosophical thought and practical life set in, we began to lose more and more the very idea of a social control, and of power to direct the development, of the most precious of all our acquirements, that of articulate speech.

I can never forget the amazement I felt when I first began my study of philology and linguistics and the origins of language, and realised this fact and its full significance. The writers one and all treated language, not as you would treat muscle, as a means of work to be brought under the most minute, elaborate and unfailing functional control, but as you might treat some distant constellation in space and its, to us, mysterious movements. . . . It does not seem to have dawned upon any one, either specialist or 'lay', what a tremendous absurdity all this way of regarding language involves.

LADY WELBY, *Significs and Language*, Ch. II, 1911.

# 3. Prose, Verse and Speech

Whether we use prose or verse on the stage, they are both but means to an end. The difference, from one point of view, is not so great as we might think. In those prose plays which survive, which are read and produced on the stage by later generations, the prose in which the characters speak is as remote, for the best part, from the vocabulary, syntax and rhythm of our ordinary speech—with its fumbling for words, its constant recourse to approximation, its disorder and its unfinished sentences—as verse is. Like verse, it has been written, and rewritten. Our two greatest prose stylists in the drama—apart from Shakespeare and the other Elizabethans who mixed prose and verse in the same play—are, I believe, Congreve and Bernard Shaw. A speech by a character of Congreve or of Shaw has—however clearly the characters may be differentiated—that unmistakable personal rhythm which is the mark of a prose style, and of which only the most accomplished conversationalists—who are for that matter monologuists—show any trace in their talk. We have all heard (too often!) of Molière's character who expressed surprise when told that he spoke prose. But it was M. Jourdain who was right, and not his mentor or his creator: he did not speak prose—he only talked. For I mean to draw a triple distinction: between prose, and verse, and our ordinary speech which is mostly below the level of either verse or prose. So if you look at it in this way, it will appear that prose, on the stage, is as artificial as verse: or alternatively, that verse can be as natural as prose.

> T. S. ELIOT, 'Poetry and Drama'; lecture delivered at Harvard University in 1950. From *On Poetry and Poets*, 1957.

# 4. Phatic Communion

A mere phrase of politeness, in use as much among savage tribes as in a European drawing-room, fulfils a function to which the meaning of its words is almost completely irrelevant. Inquiries about health, comments on weather, affirmations of some supremely obvious state of things—all such are exchanged, not in order to inform, not in this case to connect people in action, certainly not in order to express any thought. It would be even incorrect, I think, to say that such words serve the purpose of establishing a common sentiment, for this is usually absent from such current phrases of intercourse; and where it purports to exist, as in expressions of sympathy, it is avowedly spurious on one side. What is the raison d'être, therefore, of such phrases as 'How do you do?' 'Ah, here you are', 'Where do you come from?' 'Nice day today'—all of which serve in one society or another as formulae of greeting or approach?

I think that, in discussing the function of Speech in mere sociabilities, we come to one of the bedrock aspects of man's nature in society. There is in all human beings the well-known tendency to congregate, to be together, to enjoy each other's company. Many instincts and innate trends, such as fear or pugnacity, all the types of social sentiments such as ambition, vanity, passion for power and wealth, are dependent upon and associated with the fundamental tendency which makes the mere presence of others a necessity for man.

Now speech is the intimate correlate of this tendency, for, to a natural man, another man's silence is not a reassuring factor, but, on the contrary, something alarming and dangerous. The stranger who cannot speak the language is to all savage tribesmen a natural enemy. To the primitive mind, whether among savages or our own uneducated classes, taciturnity means not only unfriendliness but directly a bad character. This no doubt varies greatly with the national character but remains true as a general rule. The breaking of silence, the communion of words is the first act to establish links of fellowship, which is consummated only by the breaking of bread and the communion of food. The modern English expression, 'Nice day today' or the Melanesian phrase, 'Whence comest thou?' are needed to get over the strange and unpleasant tension which men feel when facing each other in silence.

There can be no doubt that we have here a new type of linguistic use—*phatic communion* I am tempted to call it, actuated by the demon of terminological invention—a type of speech in which ties of union are created by a mere exchange of words.

B. MALINOWSKI, 'The Problem of Meaning in Primitive Languages', supplement to C. K. Ogden and I. A. Richards, *The Meaning of Meaning*, 1923.

# 5. Gestures

Everyone is aware how strongly the gestures of the hands, expressions of the face and eyes and body reinforce the spoken exchange of thoughts and feelings. But not everyone is conscious how much the imitative and indicative gestures are subject to the various habits and usages of language communities. They, too, have a kind of historical grammar; and the natural spontaneity of such movements of expression, of communication and representation are deeply enmeshed in a system of rules that is continually developing and changing. Old French gestures differ from those of modern French; and if our powers of observation had been better trained, we should, merely from the attitudes of the faces and bodies of speakers and without hearing a single word, be able to tell their country and the nation by which their mimic language has been trained. An attempt has recently been made to regard even the permanent facial expression, the physiognomy in its typical form, as a product of the mimic and articulatory habits of language. Thus the Frankish face is different to the Suabian, not because of a difference of race, but because in it different language motor habits have become fossilized, as it were. How far such examples take us, we shall not discuss. We merely wish to point at a lower world, where a silent shadow-language lives entirely on the play of gestures, and yet in accord with language usages, through which the natural movements are trained and formed into means of understanding one another.

KARL VOSSLER, *The Spirit of Language in Civilization*, Ch. V, 1932, translated by Oscar Oeser from the German *Geist und Kultur in der Sprache*, 1925.

## 6. The Deaf and Communication

It was in the spring of 1890 that I learned to speak. The impulse to utter audible sounds had always been strong within me. I used to make noises, keeping one hand on my throat while the other hand felt the movements of my lips. I was pleased with anything that made a noise, and liked to feel the cat purr and the dog bark. I also liked to keep my hand on a singer's throat, or on a piano when it was being played. Before I lost my sight and hearing, I was fast learning to talk, but after my illness it was found that I had ceased to speak because I could not hear. . . .

No deaf child who has earnestly tried to speak the words which he has never heard—to come out of the prison of silence, where no tone of love, no song of bird, no strain of music ever pierce the stillness—can forget the thrill of surprise, the joy of discovery which came over him when he uttered his first word. Only such a one can appreciate the eagerness with which I talked to my toys, to stones, trees, birds and dumb animals, or the delight I felt when at my call Mildred ran to me or my dogs obeyed my commands. It is an unspeakable boon to me to be able to speak in winged words that need no interpretation. As I talked, happy thoughts fluttered up out of my words that might perhaps have struggled in vain to escape my fingers. . . .

Just here, perhaps, I had better explain our use of the manual alphabet, which seems to puzzle people who do not know us. One who reads or talks to me spells with his hand, using the single-hand manual alphabet generally employed by the deaf. I place my hand on the hand of the speaker so lightly as not to impede its movements. The position of the hand is as easy to feel as it is to see. I do not feel each letter, any more than you see each letter separately when you read. Constant practice makes the fingers very flexible, and some of my friends spell rapidly— about as fast as an expert writes on a typewriter. The mere spelling is, of course, no more a conscious act than it is in writing.

HELEN KELLER, *The Story of my Life*, Ch. XIII, 1903.

## 7. Advantages of Phonetics

The first and most evident advantage of phonetics is the in-
dependence it gives us. In the first place, it makes us independent
of residence abroad. Even if the learner intends to go to the
country where the language is spoken, it is a great advantage to
him to start with a thorough practical knowledge of the sounds
in which he is to practise himself.

Secondly, phonetics make us independent of native teachers.
It is certain that a phonetically trained Englishman who has a
clear knowledge of the relations between French and English
sounds can teach French sounds to English people better than
an unphonetic Frenchman—still more, an unphonetic Belgian,
Swiss, or Pole—who is unable to communicate his pronunciation
to his pupils, and perhaps speaks a vulgar or dialectal form of
French himself.

Again, phonetics enables an intelligent adult to get a sound
elementary knowledge of the sounds of a foreign language without any help from outside—that is, if he has an adequate phonetic
analysis and transcription to work with.

But the gain of a phonetic grasp of a language extends far
beyond such special considerations. A secure grasp of the sounds
of a language is a great strengthening of the mastery of its forms
and meanings. A minute discrimination of similar sounds in
closely allied languages is the surest safeguard against otherwise
inevitable confusions.

Hence also the literary and aesthetic use of phonetics.
Phonetics alone can breathe life into the dead mass of letters
which constitute a written language; it alone can bring the rustic
dialogues of our novels before every intelligent reader as living

realities, and make us realize the living power and beauty of the ancient classical languages in prose and verse.

Phonetics is not merely an indirect strengthener of grammatical associations, it is an essential part of grammar itself.

A knowledge of sentence-stress and intonation is not only an essential part of elocution and correct pronunciation, but is also an integral part of the syntax of many languages.

In short, there is no branch of the study of language which can afford to dispense with phonetics.

HENRY SWEET, *The Sounds of English*, 1908
(given there also in phonetic transcription).

# 8. Spelling Reform

Many of the advocates of spelling reform are in the habit of asserting, as if it were an axiom admitting of no dispute, that the sole function of writing is to represent sounds. It appears to me that this is one of those spurious truisms that are not intelligently believed by any one, but which continue to be repeated because nobody takes the trouble to consider what they really mean. I do not merely deny the truth of the pretended axiom as a description of the relations between speech and writing as they exist at the present day in English and other languages. I assert that, so far as peoples of literary culture are concerned, there never was a time when this formula would have correctly expressed the facts; and that it would still remain false, even if an accurately phonetic spelling had been in universal use for hundreds of years.

In order to understand distinctly the real import of the current statement, it will be well to consider the one case in which it is incontestably correct. A system of musical notation cannot perfectly fulfil its purpose unless it is so constructed that it will enable a competent musician who has mastered the system to know exactly, on looking at a composition written in the notation, what are the sounds which the composer intended his performers to produce. If a piece of written music does not attain this end with a reasonable approximation to correctness, it is useless, and might just as well not exist at all.

Now the assertion that the sole function of writing is to represent sounds amounts to saying that the case of written language is exactly parallel to that of written music. If this be so, it must follow that unless the written form of an unknown word suffices to convey a fairly correct notion of its pronunciation to a fully instructed reader, then that word might just as well not have been written at all. We shall have to say that a piece of writing is useful in the precise degree in which it is phonetically spelt, and no further. Perhaps no one will venture to say that this statement is in accord with the facts; but unless the current pseudo-axiom means this, I am at a loss to imagine what it *can* mean. The truth is that between written music and written language there is one all-important difference. In written music the representation of sounds is the absolute ultimate end. In written language it is only a means. We use visible symbols for the sounds of speech because spoken sounds are symbols of meaning. The ultimate end, and for most purposes, though not for all, the only important end, of written language is to convey meaning. Now the degree in which a piece of writing or print is capable of conveying its meaning does not at all necessarily depend on the accuracy with which it suggests the sounds that would have been heard if the composition had been spoken instead of written.

HENRY BRADLEY, *Spoken and Written Language*, 1913.

# 9. Phonetic Analysis

A real analysis of the word into its proper elements is not merely extremely difficult, but is actually impossible. A word is not a united compound of a definite number of independent sounds, of which each can be expressed by an alphabetical sign; but it is essentially a continuous series of infinitely numerous sounds, and alphabetical symbols do no more than bring out certain characteristic points of this series in an imperfect way. The remainder, which remains undenoted, no doubt necessarily reveals itself from the definition of these points, but reveals itself only up to a certain point. The continuity of sound is seen with the greatest clearness in the case of the so-called diphthongs, which exhibit such a series of very numerous elements. . . . But it follows from this continuity of the word that an idea of the individual parts cannot be a self-yielded result, but must be the fruit of scientific reflection, however primitive this may be, and it is the practical need of writing to express sounds which has conduced to this.

HERMANN PAUL, *Principles of the History of Language*, 1891, Ch. III, translated by H. A. Strong from the second edition of *Principien der Sprachgeschichte*, 1886.

# 10. Metre in Prose

Metre, in the primary degree of a simple series of isochronous intervals, marked by accents, is as natural to spoken language as an even pace is natural to walking. Prose delivery, without this amount of metre, is like a drunkard's walk, the irregularity of which is so far from being natural to a person in his senses, that it is not even to be imitated without effort. Now, as dancing is no more than an increase of the element of measure which already exists in walking, so verse is but an additional degree of that metre which is inherent in prose speaking. . . .

The metrical and musical law in prose has been disregarded and forgotten, because its nature is so simple that its observance may safely be trusted to instinct, and requires no aid from typographical divisions. Probably many of my readers will feel as much surprised at learning that they have been speaking in metre all their lives, as the *Bourgeois Gentilhomme* felt on being told that he was, without instruction, in the habit of talking prose. I certainly cannot expect them to believe so startling a proposition upon my mere assertion: I must allege a few proofs, premising, however, that the *melody*, or element of *tone* in language, is so inseparably connected with its *metre* or *time*, that the two things will scarcely consent to be considered separately. By the metre and melody of prose, I of course mean the metre and melody which exists in the common and intelligible delivery of it. Verse itself is only verse on the condition of right reading: we may, if we choose, read the most perfect verse so that all the effect of verse shall be lost. The same thing may be done with prose. We may clearly articulate all the syllables, and preserve their due connection in the phrases they constitute; and yet, by neglecting to give them their relative tones, and to group them according to time, convert them from prose into something nameless, absurd, and unintelligible. So far is it from being true that the time and tone of prose reading and speaking are without law, that their laws are more strict than those of grammar itself. There are never two equally good ways of reading a sentence, though there may be half a dozen of writing it. If one and the same sentence is readable in more than one way, it is because it has more than one possible meaning. 'Shall you walk out today?' is a question which may be asked with as many variations of stress and tone as there are words in it; but every variation involves a variation of meaning.

> COVENTRY PATMORE, Essay on English Metrical Law, 1856 (reprinted in Vol. II of the second collective edition of Patmore's *Poems*, 1886).

# 11. Poetry Spoken and Written

When, therefore, we consider the phonetic aspect of poetry, it is obvious that we assume the spoken existence of language; so obvious that it might hardly seem worth mentioning. But we are sometimes apt to forget, even in this connexion, that language has, and has had for many centuries, a double life, in poetry as elsewhere. Language lives as the spoken word, and it lives also as the written (or printed) word. The spoken word cannot be anything else than sound accepted as the symbol of an idea; and the written word was originally the symbol of this spoken sound: that is to say, the symbol of the symbol of an idea. But the written word can be, and has long since in part become, something else than the symbol of a symbol; it can be a symbol in its own right. For the human mind will always short-circuit a process when it can. As soon as the habit of *reading to oneself* was established, the second-hand symbolism of the written word was short-circuited; and the written word became itself the symbol of the idea, without having to pass through the symbolism of sound. Printing has fixed this short-circuit in our civilised mentality so deeply that many of us are scarcely aware of it.

Language, as communicable symbolism of ideas, has two modes of existence: it exists as audible signs and it exists as visible signs. Generally, the only practical relation between the two kinds of signs is that they both refer to the same thing: the English we read has almost given up pretending to have anything to do with the English we hear. As a rule, when we are reading to ourselves, the printed word refers immediately to its idea; the sound of the word very likely comes in, but it is not required, and may be due to association with the idea as much as to taking the

110

letters as phonetic signs. The sound of the word at any rate only comes in as a faint unnecessary accompaniment, to which we only attend as a sort of mild corroboration. But, though it may be proper enough to read our newspapers in that style, it will not do for poetry. Poetry consists absolutely of the word spoken and heard: the printed word must always be frankly the symbol of articulate sound. We must hear what the poet has to say; if we are reading to ourselves, we must hear it mentally. Otherwise we shall miss half his technique; and that means, we shall miss half of what he is trying to express.

But there is still something to be said on this matter; the visible word is not to be dismissed in poetry altogether, in favour of the audible word. There is no doubt, in fact, that the existence of language as printed words has had a profound influence on the art of poetry, though it would take too long to investigate this here exactly. We read poetry to ourselves more often than hear it read aloud; and poets, consciously or not, have taken advantage of this. Poetry will always take advantage of anything that will increase or refine its expressive power. I said, that the printed word in poetry must *always* be taken as a symbol of an articulate sound. I did not say, it could *only* be taken so. When we read poetry to ourselves, it is not, I think, the usual thing to refer the word to the sound and thence, *through* the sound, to the idea; I think rather we refer the printed word immediately to the idea and simultaneously to the sound as well. And this is important; for eye-language is a much subtler and nimbler affair than ear-language. We can get, in printed language, in the appeal through the eye, a more instant and more certain apprehension of fine associations of ideas, of delicate shades of significance, than you can ever get through the ear.

LASCELLES ABERCROMBIE, *The Theory of Poetry*, Ch. V, 1924.

## 12. Good English

Good English is plain, easy, and smooth in the mouth of an un-affected English gentleman. A studied and factitious pronuncia-tion, which requires perpetual attention, and imposes perpetual constraint, is exceedingly disgusting. A small intermixture of provincial peculiarities may, perhaps, have an agreeable effect, as the notes of different birds concur in the harmony of the grove, and please more than if they were all exactly alike. I could name some gentlemen of Ireland, to whom a slight pro-portion of the accent and recitative of that country is an advan-tage. The same observations will apply to the gentlemen of Scot-land. I do not mean that we should speak as broad as a certain prosperous member of parliament from that country; though it has been well observed, that 'it has been of no small use to him, as it rouses the attention of the House by its uncommonness; and is equal to tropes and figures in a good English speaker'. I would give as an instance of what I mean to recommend to my country-men, the pronunciation of the late Sir Gilbert Elliot; and may I presume to add that of the present Earl of Marchmont, who told me, with great good humour, that the master of a shop in Lon-don, where he was not known, said to him, 'I suppose, Sir, you are an American.' 'Why so, Sir?' said his Lordship. 'Because, Sir,' replied the shopkeeper, 'you speak neither English nor Scotch, but something different from both, which I conclude is the language of America.'

JAMES BOSWELL, *The Life of Samuel Johnson*, 1791.

# 13. Henry Sweet

The English have no respect for their language, and will not teach their children to speak it. They cannot spell it because they have nothing to spell it with but an old foreign alphabet of which only the consonants—and not all of them—have any agreed speech value. Consequently no man can teach himself what it should sound like from reading it; and it is impossible for an Englishman to open his mouth without making some other Englishman despise him. Most European languages are now accessible in black and white to foreigners; English and French are not thus accessible even to Englishmen and Frenchmen. The reformer we need most today is an energetic enthusiast: that is why I have made such a one the hero of a popular play.

There have been heroes of that kind crying in the wilderness for many years past. When I became interested in the subject towards the end of the eighteen-seventies, the illustrious Alexander Melville Bell, the inventor of Visible Speech, had emigrated to Canada, where his son invented the telephone; but Alexander J. Ellis was still a London patriarch, with an impressive head always covered by a velvet skull cap, for which he would apologize to public meetings in a very courtly manner. He and Tito Pagliardini, another phonetic veteran, were men whom it was impossible to dislike. Henry Sweet, then a young man lacked their sweetness of character: he was about as conciliatory to conventional mortals as Ibsen or Samuel Butler. His great ability as a phonetician (he was, I think, the best of them all at his job) would have entitled him to high official recognition, and perhaps enabled him to popularize his subject, but for his Satanic contempt for all academic dignitaries and persons in general who thought more of Greek than of phonetics. . . .

Pygmalion Higgins is not a portrait of Sweet, to whom the adventure of Eliza Doolittle would have been impossible; still, as will be seen, there are touches of Sweet in the play. With Higgins's physique and temperament Sweet might have set the Thames on fire. As it was, he impressed himself professionally on Europe to an extent that made his comparative personal obscurity, and the failure of Oxford to do justice to his eminence, a puzzle to foreign specialists in his subject.

BERNARD SHAW, *Pygmalion*; Preface to
Penguin edition, 1941.

## 14. Linguistic Tolerance

We must learn to become more tolerant of the word as spoken by Americans, Canadians, Australians, and South Africans; and English-speaking listeners on the other side of the world's oceans must remember that when it comes to throwing stones at the so-called British English, they, too, live in glass houses. The English language is a very much more widespread language than the world has yet seen in its history, and the first thing the English-speaking peoples have to learn is that there are many good ways of speaking it. Everybody believes his own to be the best, an attitude that, in other spheres of life, civilization has taught us to despise. Many national misunderstandings are due to simple language differences, as even a short comparative investigation into English and American intonation will convince anybody. Many Americans are offended by the normal intonations of British English, just as Britishers are often hurt by American intonations. Much of our hasty generalization concerning the French temperament is due to the fact that French speakers use, in normal circumstances, types of intonation that are in English associated with situations that are not normal. . . . We are all so susceptible to the minutest details of speech behaviour, that whenever we observe the speech behaviour of others, we imagine them to be suffering from the same emotions as we should have to suffer from before we behaved as they do. And as a rule, it is the intonation that hurts; English spoken on Swedish intonation may sound petulant, on Russian intonation lugubrious, on German intonation offensive, on French intonation argumentative, on many American intonations casual or cocksure, on Danish intonation flat and sombre. . . . What foreign languages sound like when spoken on British or American speech rhythms and intonations is best left to a lively imagination; many of the popular opinions held by foreign nations of the Englishman are due to English intonations, which may suggest offensive haughtiness or impudence to people who habitually use other intonations. And the loud voice in which many English and American men and women are in the habit of conducting private conversation in public places may have more serious consequences than that of ruffling conductors in Covent Garden. The volume of offence that it causes on the mainland of Europe would be hard to measure.

This, perhaps, is the greatest danger of the spoken word; the technical details of its utterance, of little significance to the speaker, may arouse in the minds of listeners emotions far different from those that prompt it in the mind of the speaker. Indeed it may be that the printed word is safer for international currency until the world has learnt, if not to standardize the relation between emotion and intonation, at any rate to behave in the international linguistic playground less like the babies in an Infants' School playground.

A. LLOYD JAMES, *The Broadcast Word*, Ch. I, 1935 (some sentences omitted, and the order of some others changed).

## 15. The Story of Arthur the Rat

There was once a young rat named Arthur, who would never take the trouble to make up his mind. Whenever his friends asked him if he would like to go out with them, he would only answer, 'I don't know.' He wouldn't say 'yes', and he wouldn't say 'no' either. He could never learn to make a choice.

His aunt Helen said to him, 'No one will ever care for you if you carry on like this. You have no more mind than a blade of grass.' Arthur looked wise, but said nothing.

One rainy day the rats heard a great noise in the loft where they lived. The pine rafters were all rotten, and at last one of the joists had given way and fallen to the ground. The walls shook, and all the rats' hair stood on end with fear and horror. 'This won't do,' said the old rat who was chief. 'I'll send out scouts to search for a new home.'

Three hours later the seven scouts came back and said, 'We have found a stone house which is just what we wanted: there is room and good food for us all. There is a kindly horse named Nelly, a cow, a calf, and a garden with an elm tree.' Just then the old rat caught sight of young Arthur. 'Are you coming with us?' he asked. 'I don't know,' Arthur sighed, 'the roof may not come down just yet.' 'Well,' said the old rat angrily, 'we can't wait all day for you to make up your mind. Right about face! March!' And they went off.

Arthur stood and watched the other rats hurry away. The idea of an immediate decision was too much for him. 'I'll go back to my hole for a bit,' he said to himself, 'just to make up my mind.'

That night there was a great crash that shook the earth, and down came the whole roof. Next day some men rode up and looked at the ruins. One of them moved a board, and under it they saw a young rat lying on his side, quite dead, half in and half out of his hole.

After HENRY SWEET, *Primer of Spoken English*, 1890.

## 16. The North Wind and the Sun

The North Wind and the Sun were disputing which was the stronger, when a traveller came along wrapped in a warm cloak. They agreed that the one who first succeeded in making the traveller take his cloak off should be considered stronger than the other. Then the North Wind blew as hard as he could, but the more he blew the more closely did the traveller fold his cloak around him; and at last the North Wind gave up the attempt. Then the Sun shone out warmly, and immediately the traveller took off his cloak. And so the North Wind was obliged to confess that the Sun was the stronger of the two.

*The Principles of the International Phonetic Association*, 1912 (and subsequent editions).

## 17. A Model English Phonetic Text

Those who have at times found it necessary, for one reason or another, to produce a specimen text in phonetic transcription will have experienced a difficulty in selecting a suitable passage. To be ideally suitable it should fulfil four requirements. It should

(1) contain all the symbols,

(2) exemplify the chief phenomena of weakening, shortening, stress, word-linking, etc.,

(3) make sense,

(4) be as short as possible.

Now if we select a passage at random from any book, before our conditions (1), (2) and (3) are fulfilled, the text does not fulfil condition (4). On the other hand, if we restrict our passage in order for it to conform to condition (4) it will not fulfil conditions (1), (2) and (3).

The following passage is an essay towards finding a text which the most nearly fulfils the four requirements. . . .

At what time are you going to the exhibition? I thought I heard you tell your brother this morning that you expected to meet him there at about two.

Yes. Would you like to join us there?

I would, with pleasure, but I am not sure whether I can. In any case I must leave early to catch the four train. I do not live here now; I live in the suburbs and I want to get home before it is dark.

Are you really in such a hurry to get home? Must you? If it is solely on that account, we can take you back in our car.

Can you? That will be splendid! All right.

HAROLD E. PALMER, *A Few Documents on English Phonetic Notation*, Tokyo, 1925.

# List of References and Works Consulted

[Note on *Le Maître Phonétique*: the actual name of this periodical, as it appears on the title-page of each issue, is printed in phonetic transcription, and it will be referred to below by the familar abbreviation of the transcribed form of its name, *m.f.* References to contributions are given by the *year* and the *page*, which will be found adequate for locating them (there is no numbering of volumes, and although each issue has its own serial number, this often appears only on the outside cover, which may easily become detached, or in bound volumes may have been removed). Titles of articles are here cited in normal orthography, though as published they usually appear in phonetic transcription.]

ABERCROMBIE, DAVID (1953), 'Phonetic transcriptions', *m.f.*, pp. 32–34.
— (1954), 'The recording of dialect material', *Orbis*, Vol. III, pp. 231–5.
— (1956), *Problems and Principles*. Longmans, Green and Co. Ltd., London.
ARMSTRONG, L. E. (1923), *An English Phonetic Reader*. University of London Press Ltd.
— and WARD, I. C. (1931), *A Handbook of English Intonation*. W. Heffer and Sons Ltd., Cambridge, and B. G. Teubner, Leipzig.
BATCHELOR, T. (1809), *An Orthoëpical Analysis of the English Language*. Didier and Tebbett, London.

# List of references and works consulted

BLOOMFIELD, L. (1935), *Language*. George Allen and Unwin Ltd., London.

BROOK, G. L. (1935), *An English Phonetic Reader*. Manchester University Press.

BROWN, R. GRANT (1932), 'Broad transcription', *m.f.*, pp. 78–80.

— (1935), 'Broad transcription', *m.f.*, pp. 65–66.

— (1942), 'Broad transcription', *m.f.*, 19–21.

— (1953), 'Broad transcription', *m.f.*, pp. 16–18.

CAMP, L. SPRAGUE DE (1946), 'What is narrowness?', *m.f.*, pp. 17–20.

CHAO, Y. R. (1933), 'The non-uniqueness of phonemic solutions of phonetic systems', *Bulletin of the National Research Institute of History and Philology of the Academia Sinica*, Vol. IV, pp. 363–97; now available in M. Joos, *Readings in Linguistics*, American Council of Learned Societies, Washington, 1957.

CHAPALLAZ, M., *Specimens of English in Phonetic Transcription*. n.d. Printed for the Department of Phonetics, University College, London, for private circulation.

DAVIES, H. H. (1938), *The Mollusc*. Annotated Phonetic Edition with Tone-Marks by Dorothée Palmer. W. Heffer and Sons Ltd., Cambridge.

DUMVILLE, B. (1909), *The Science of Speech*. University Tutorial Press Ltd., London (2nd edn., 1926).

*English Phonetic Reader*. n.d. Printed for the Department of Phonetics, University College, London, for private circulation.

ENKVIST, N. E. (1955), book review in *m.f.*, p. 42.

GIMSON, A. C. (1945–9), 'Implications of the phonemic/chronemic groupings of English vowels', *Acta Linguistica*, Vol. V, pp. 94–100.

I[nternational] P[honetic] A[ssociation], *Exposé des Principes* (1900). Bourg-la-Reine, France (2nd edn., 1905. 3rd edn., 1908).

—, *Aim and Principles of the* (1904). Bourg-la-Reine, France.

—, *Principles of the* (1912). Bourg-la-Reine and London.

## List of references and works consulted

—, *Principles of the* (1949). University College, London (reprinted 1962).

JASSEM, W. (1950), 'Phonemic Transcription of the Vowels of Educated Southern English', *m.f.*, pp. 10–12.

— (1952), *Intonation of Conversational English*. Wroclaw.

JONES, D. (1907), *Phonetic Transcriptions of English Prose*. Clarendon Press, Oxford (2nd edn., 1914).

— (1909), *The Pronunciation of English*. Cambridge University Press (2nd edn., 1914. 3rd edn., 1950. 4th edn., 1956).

— (1912), *Phonetic Readings in English*. Carl Winter, Heidelberg (many subsequent editions).

— (1917), *An English Pronouncing Dictionary*. J. M. Dent and Sons Ltd., London (11th edn., Everyman's Reference Library, 1956).

— (1918), *An Outline of English Phonetics*. Teubner, Leipzig (3rd edn., W. Heffer and Sons Ltd., Cambridge, 1932. 8th edn., 1956. Other editions are merely reprints with small changes).

— (1931), text in 'Partie des élèves', *m.f.*, p. 12.

— (1950), *The Phoneme*. W. Heffer and Sons Ltd., Cambridge (2nd edn., 1962).

LAWRENSON, A. C. (1935), 'On the broad transcription of Southern English', *m.f.*, pp. 22–24.

MACCARTHY, P. A. D. (1944), *English Pronunciation*. W. Heffer and Sons Ltd., Cambridge.

— (1945), *An English Pronouncing Vocabulary*. W. Heffer and Sons Ltd., Cambridge.

— (1956*a*), *English Conversation Reader*. Longmans, Green and Co. Ltd., London.

— (1956*b*), 'Phonetic transcription: an attempt at clarification', *English Language Teaching*, Vol. X, pp. 61–65.

MACKENZIE, C. F., and DREW, P. W. (1919), *A Phonetic Reader for Use in Junior Classes*. Manchester University Press.

MARTINET, ANDRÉ (1946), 'Savoir pourquoi et pour qui l'on transcrit', *m.f.*, pp. 14–17.

NOEL-ARMFIELD, G. (1914), *English Humour in Phonetic Transcript*. W. Heffer and Sons Ltd., Cambridge (2nd edn., 1919).

## List of references and works consulted

O'CONNOR, J. D. (1948), *New Phonetic Readings*. Berne.

PALMER, DOROTHÉE. See H. H. Davies (1938).

PALMER, H. E. (1925), *A Few Documents on English Phonetic Notation*. Institute for Research in English Teaching, Tokyo.

PASSY, P. (1926), 'A propos de nouveaux signes', *m.f.*, p. 13.

— (1932), 'Transcription anglaise', *m.f.*, p. 50.

PETERSON, H. (1936), 'The transcription of English', *m.f.*, pp. 10–11.

PRING, J. T. (1947), 'What transcription is best for teaching pronunciation?', *m.f.*, pp. 24–27.

— and GERMER, R. (1962), *A New English Phonetic Reader*. Dortmund.

RIPMAN, WALTER (1908), *Specimens of English*. J. M. Dent and Sons Ltd. (many subsequent editions).

ŠČERBA, L. (1911), *Court exposé de la prononciation russe*. International Phonetic Association.

SCHOCH, ALFRED D. (1907), 'Uniform writing or simplified alphabet, which?', *m.f.*, pp. 80–84.

SCOTT, N. C. (1941), 'Broad transcription', *m.f.*, pp. 48–51.

— (1942), *English Conversations in Simplified Phonetic Transcription*. W. Heffer and Sons Ltd., Cambridge.

SMITH, HERBERT (1908), *Transcriptions of Shindler's Echo of Spoken English*. N. G. Elwert, Marburg.

*Specimens of English in Simplified Phonetic Transcription*. n.d. Printed for the Department of Phonetics, University College, London.

SWEET, HENRY (1890), *A Primer of Spoken English*. Clarendon Press, Oxford.

— (1908), *The Sounds of English*. Clarendon Press, Oxford.

— (1911), 'Phonetics', *Encyclopaedia Britannica*, 11th edn., Vol. XXI, pp. 458–67. Cambridge University Press.

TIBBITTS, E. L. (1946), *A Phonetic Reader for Foreign Learners of English*. W. Heffer and Sons Ltd., Cambridge.

TRAGER, G. L. (1935), 'The transcription of English', *m.f.*, pp. 10–13.

— and BLOCH, B. (1941), 'The syllabic phonemes of English', *Language*, Vol. XVII, pp. 223–46.

## List of references and works consulted

ULDALL, H. J. (1933), *A Danish Phonetic Reader*. University of London Press Ltd.

WARD, IDA C. (1923), *Defects of Speech*. J. M. Dent and Sons Ltd., London (2nd edn., 1929).

— (1929), *The Phonetics of English*. W. Heffer and Sons Ltd., Cambridge (2nd edn., 1931. 3rd edn., 1939. 4th edn., 1945).